I0048854

PRAISE FOR

MARKETING IN THE (GREAT, BIG, MESSY) REAL WORLD

"The real world is indeed a messy place, and success in navigating it depends on bringing the right mindset to the effort. Kathleen Schaub does a superb job of weaning us away from the false allure of deterministic operating models of a prior era of industrial automation to instead embrace more agile approaches to our ever-changing, digitally transforming marketplace. Marketers must still maintain a foundational commitment to accountability, but they, and their funding sponsors, must understand they are working with probabilities, not certainties, which calls for constant iteration and course-correcting—*better, better, better . . . never best.*"

—Geoffrey Moore, author of *Crossing the Chasm* and *Zone to Win*

"Kathleen Schaub is no stranger to the battle for customer mindshare and market share in a digitally connected economy. A veteran of Silicon Valley and beyond, she delivers a timely treatise for the AI-powered marketing era with a call for collective, on-demand intelligence in the enterprise and agile operation by cross-functional, integrated teams. Perhaps marketing today has to resemble modern warfare relying on automated drone oversight and real-time data feeds to guide adaptive, predictive, and opportunistic tactical action in the field."

—Donovan Neale-May, executive director, CMO Council

"Marketing is complex and uncertain. Rather than wish that away, Kathleen Schaub shows how to strategically harness that reality to your advantage. She has delivered an insightful and thought-provoking playbook for how marketing teams can embrace the great, big, messy real world and thrive in it. A must-read for today's marketing leader."

—**Scott Brinker,** editor, chiefmartec

"Kathleen brilliantly shatters the fallacy that marketing can be managed like a simple machine. By reframing marketing as a complex, non-linear system, she explains why our old playbooks aren't working and provides a road map for navigating the uncertainty rather than fighting it. What makes *Marketing in the (Great, Big, Messy) Real World* so great is how Schaub manages to be both erudite but also practical, serving up real advice for putting systems thinking into action: treating marketing as an investment and not a cost center, accepting uncertainty, building more connected organizational structures, and creating intelligence systems that can sense the market. For marketing leaders scratching their heads over unpredictable results despite all their best efforts, this book doesn't just explain why—it shows you a better way forward."

—**Jon Miller,** B2B expert and cofounder of Marketo and Engagio

"I've had the privilege of working with Kathleen over the years. In this essential guide, she reveals how traditional management practices often worsen the very challenges executives are trying to solve. Rather than following traditional strategies, Schaub blends design thinking, data analytics, and mindfulness to equip marketing teams to move beyond outdated models and thrive in volatile environments. With her guidance, marketing leaders can gain the agility and strategic foresight needed for long-term success. She's also an exceptional storyteller; this is a must-read!"

—**Holly Rollo,** former CMO, author of *Power of Surge,*
CEO of Surge Strategies

"Kathleen Schaub's new book *Marketing in the (Great, Big, Messy) Real World* is a primer on the new rules of the game that are barreling down the road fast. The shift that her book so eloquently calls for is happening now for three big reasons: the rise of causal AI as the GPS for marketing and sales, the changes in judicial rulings mandating a much broader and more inclusive definition of fiduciary duty, and a fundamental shift in the balance of power between vendors and customers. To navigate this, teams and leaders have to see going to market as a network of many causes and effects. They must be bookies, using their view into causality to place better bets and make better decisions. Kathleen tells it like it is, and if you don't listen to what she says in this new and provocative book, *you'll wish you had.*"

—**Mark Stouse,** CEO of ProofAnalytics.ai and FIDUCIARI.ai

MARKETING

in the

(GREAT, BIG, MESSY)

REAL WORLD

REWIRE YOUR MARKETING ORGANIZATION
TO NAVIGATE ANYTHING

KATHLEEN SCHAUB

RIVER GROVE
BOOKS

This publication is designed to provide accurate and authoritative information in regard to the subject matter covered. It is sold with the understanding that the publisher and author are not engaged in rendering legal, accounting, or other professional services. Nothing herein shall create an attorney-client relationship, and nothing herein shall constitute legal advice or a solicitation to offer legal advice. If legal advice or other expert assistance is required, the services of a competent professional should be sought.

Published by River Grove Books
Austin, TX
www.rivergrovebooks.com

Copyright © 2025 Kathleen Schaub

All rights reserved.

Thank you for purchasing an authorized edition of this book and for complying with copyright law. No part of this book may be reproduced, stored in a retrieval system, or transmitted by any means, electronic, mechanical, photocopying, recording, or otherwise, without written permission from the copyright holder.

For permission to reprint copyrighted material, grateful acknowledgment is made to:
Thot Leader Labs: Figure 7.1, Marketing Attribution is Fake

Distributed by River Grove Books

Design and composition by Greenleaf Book Group
Cover design by Greenleaf Book Group
Cover image used under license from Adobestock.com

Publisher's Cataloging-in-Publication data is available.

Print ISBN: 978-1-63299-986-3

eBook ISBN: 978-1-63299-987-0

First Edition

To my husband Bill, my constant supporter and coach.
And to the hundreds of marketers, colleagues, mentors,
and clients, who have been with me on this path.
Thank you for your time and wisdom. May the
winds of change always be at your back.

CONTENTS

MARKETING IS NOT A VENDING MACHINE

*The capacity to tolerate complexity and welcome contradiction,
not the need for simplicity and certainty, is the attribute of
an explorer . . . Curiously, it was by abandoning the search
for absolute truth that science began to make progress.*

—Heinz Pagels, *American physicist*

Everyone loves a vending machine. Put money in, press a button, and out pops your favorite snack. With vending machines, we can easily explore multiple options and compare before buying. We love vending machines for their speed, convenience, exceptional efficiency, 24/7 accessibility—and for their predictability.

Wouldn't it be wonderful if marketing were like that? If you could get your desired revenue surge whenever you bought advertising, if the number of webinar attendees could forecast pipeline value, or if managers could compare campaign options so conveniently?

Enterprises would settle for even a fraction of this machine-like reliability. Every CEO and CFO that I know keenly desires a more predictable and controllable marketing function. The urgency to make marketing work well and to reliably produce greater return on investment (ROI) has intensified in the digital era as in-person sales and retail opportunities have diminished.

But marketing has never worked deterministically and never will. Instead, predicting outcomes from marketing actions is more like forecasting what the weather will be like. Even tomorrow's weather is somewhat uncertain, and the weather a few months from now is, at best, a probability. Although different in scope, a similar lack of deterministic predictability is prevalent in sales and marketing. Let me give you an example.

A US Navy submarine cruising on a routine mission one day suffered the failure of a piece of networking equipment and needed to replace it quickly. The technician in charge conducted research online: comparing products, viewing technical service information, exchanging emails with knowledgeable colleagues, and checking approved vendor lists. He selected a product, contacted a reseller in an African port city, purchased the technology, and arranged for installation. This whole process took place within days and went so smoothly that the networking equipment supplier wasn't aware of the story until months later when a salesperson landed a "blue bird" deal: a multimillion-dollar commitment from the Navy that popped up without notice. The success of that oceanic purchase had inspired the bigger contract.

This revenue could not have been forecasted. Many contributing elements of the sale were random, including the circumstances that caused the older equipment to break down and the coincidental location of the submarine when failure occurred. The technician had not been a particular target of previous marketing efforts. And although the equipment vendor had captured a few data points in their marketing systems and could later reconstruct parts of the buyer's trail, that information represented only the proverbial tip of the iceberg of what was happening behind the scenes.

Largely invisible customer journeys like this one happen every day. Every marketer (and every salesperson) can reel off more examples. There is nothing vending machine–like about these stories, and that's the crux of the challenge I address in this book.

The difficulty of managing in such an uncertain and ambiguous environment creates persistent challenges for marketing leaders and their executive partners. Here are just a few examples:

- Deficits in customer experience

- Conflicts between marketing and sales over leads

- Power struggles over who's in charge and who's adding value

- Controversy over whether to spend marketing funds on short-term or long-term tactics

- The incessant inability to showcase ROI from marketing efforts

This last challenge, ambiguous ROI, is particularly thorny, and it drives a wedge between marketing leaders and the C-suite executives who make financial decisions. Without the ability to predict marketing outcomes, how can managers compare investments across the business portfolio or determine the business impact of increasing or cutting the marketing budget? How can they decide whether to weight spending to stimulate short-term (but fleeting) demand versus the longer-term (but more lasting) benefits of brand?

The desire for vending machine predictability drives the deterministic questions that marketing leaders have grown to expect from company executives, such as:

- "How much more revenue can we get if we give you another $20,000 in budget?"

- "What will the pipeline impact be if you hire another marketer?"

- "What's the *one* best program you conduct?"

These questions, along with dozens of other requests for certainty and assurance seem reasonable, given the increase in data and analytics tools available to marketers today. Yet, determining the answers to these kinds of questions, especially within the context of long sales cycles, has failed. The toll on CMOs is evident with their average turnover being the shortest in the C-suite at three and a half years and continuing to decrease, according to major recruiting company, Korn Ferry.[1]

Sound familiar? These issues haunted marketing executives when I was a chief marketing officer (CMO). More recently, as a leader in market research firm International Data Corporation's (IDC) CMO Advisory practice, I encountered these conundrums in hundreds of companies from major brands to fledgling start-ups. As I researched these challenges, I discovered why they are so persistent and found approaches to avoid or overcome them. I wrote this book to share these findings with CMOs, other marketing leaders, and their C-suite partners.

THE NEED FOR COMPLEXITYWISE MARKETING

The juxtaposition of the two examples given above—the weirdness of customer journeys and the demand by the C-suite for deterministic marketing outcomes—captures the conundrum that chief marketing officers face today. They are dealing with an increasingly complex world where factors affecting sales are often unpredictable, yet they are expected to operate their departments like predictable, well-oiled machines.

Stewart Brand, author of *The Clock of the Long Now,*[2] said, "When a design problem resists solution, reframe the problem in such a way that it invites solution."[3] I believe that the answer to breaking through marketing's persistent problems lies in reframing marketing management to accept and embrace the market's uncertainty and complexity. That's what this book is about.

The necessary reframing didn't arrive for me in a single "aha" moment. Instead, over the past few decades, I had become increasingly aware of the dissonance surrounding the idea of marketing's persistent challenges. Never has marketing had more tracking data and measuring technology available. Yet at the same time, marketing seems to be getting more frantic and harder to comprehend. For a long time, I couldn't square these two truths. Gradually, a series of experiences shone a brighter and finally glaring light on what I came to understand is a fundamental misunderstanding about marketing's reality.

The path to this realization started when I worked as a marketer in technology retail, smack in the middle of a sprawling supply chain, which gave me an early window into the challenges inherent in such a complex environment. Studying Just-in Time (JIT) inventory management and the work of W. Edwards Deming, an eminent American engineer, professor, author, and statistician, was a big eye-opener. Deming is best known for his work in Japan, where he strongly influenced the revolutionary statistical controls that eventually gave rise to practices such as Lean Management and Agile methodologies. At nearly the same time, I recall listening to an audio version of Peter Senge's ground-breaking book about systems thinking, *The Fifth Discipline*,[4] while working out on a stationary bicycle. Senge was sharing a simulation of inventory problems in a multicompany supply chain. At one point I screamed (in my head), "Don't do it!" to Senge's example of manufacturers who overproduce in response to natural ups and downs in store sales. As time went on, I was introduced to what was once called *chaos theory* along with its strange attributes and implications. Much research has been done to develop systems thinking and in the field of complexity science since then, and as I learned more, I began to recognize familiar patterns.

Finally, it hit me. The origin of marketing's persistent problems lies not with crummy CMOs, combative CFOs, or unreasonable CEOs. The problem springs from the gross discrepancy between the uncertain, constantly changing complexity of marketing and the mechanical way business tries to manage the function.

Conventional business practices and structures are often barriers to agility and can degrade market system health. To thrive in the digitally transformed market, companies must adopt mindsets and methods markedly different from those designed for the industrial era. I coined the term *ComplexityWise* to characterize new ways of thinking and managing that foster market system health along with the agility required for effectiveness in marketing's complex and sometimes messy reality.

The mind shifts and capabilities described in this book are those I found most frequently when researching the success of leaders in turbulent environments as well as within the recommendations from pioneering consultants, academics, and technology companies. Consider this playbook to be a living collection of recommended guidance, not a best practices recipe book. We are still discovering and refining approaches to thrive in complex systems and even the most successful, dependable plays must occasionally be set aside when the situation warrants.

When applied to marketing, ComplexityWise thinking activates the human potential for problem-solving while leveraging technology to augment human capabilities. Technology is a major contributor to why we even know how complexity operates, and it is fundamental to ComplexityWise marketing at scale. By working with marketing's complexity instead of ignoring it, companies will realize more value.

BEING SUCCESSFUL IN A COMPLEX SYSTEM

Marketing, like stock markets and the weather, is what scientists call a *complex system*. Interactions between consumers, buying groups, and enterprises, each of whom is a singular blend of motivations, preferences, desires, and behaviors, create feedback loops that produce many unknowns and introduce uncertainty into every situation. Digital technology has only increased and accelerated these interactions, compounding complexity's effects. Marketing is more like raising a child than operating a machine. Any sphere where humans interact shares these characteristics.

If marketing is not—and will never be—even close to a predictable vending machine, where does that leave us?

While business continues to struggle to bring marketing's uncertainty under control, other leaders working in a broad range of turbulent environments have taken a different approach. They acknowledge the complexity of their operating environments and, aided by science and technology, set out to discover and develop approaches purpose-built for working in this reality.

In this book, I've done the same for marketing. I've collected the best mindsets and methods that I found in the multiple disciplines that must deal with unpredictability and complexity: software developers, military leaders, first responders, academics, sports and gaming franchises, stock market investors, social scientists, naturalists, and healthcare professionals, as well as forward-looking businesses.

The playbook is divided into three sections:

- **Part I: Where We Are, How We Got There, and Where We Need to Go** has two chapters. They provide a brief review of common management philosophies—most of which first became prominent in the early twentieth century—that have influenced how marketing management is conducted today. The chapters discuss why those traditional approaches are outdated and give an overview of the mind shifts and operational capabilities needed for success in today's world.

- **Part II: Embracing Complexity—Four Mind Shifts:** Mind shifts describe ways of *thinking* that will help CMOs embrace the reality of complex marketing environments. If industrial-era models are inappropriate, what replaces them? These four chapters answer that question, reframing the traditional "marketing as a machine" paradigm into more useful perspectives inspired by other complex, unpredictable environments.

- **Part III: Engaging Complexity—Operational Shifts:** Once ComplexityWise mindsets become activated, enterprises will incline toward management methods that improve marketing's ability to engage with the fast-paced, uncertain world. ComplexityWise marketing involves making adaptations to teams, organizations, culture, processes, and information systems. The capabilities are presented as directive practices because effort is continual and there is no destination that signals arrival.

In short, what you'll find in this book is a guide to developing the essential capabilities that CMOs and all marketing leaders need to ensure that their team delivers trusted outcomes in an era of increasing complexity. You'll learn why some conventional management practices aggravate the very problems that executives hope to alleviate and how by reframing marketing as a complex system you will find the concrete steps to make your organization more effective.

I'll set your expectations up front. ComplexityWise marketing isn't a recipe or a list of five things you can do to succeed. But neither are these mindsets and practices outrageous or unheard of. Some elements will produce results within weeks while others need time to ripen. Executives will recognize some and may find they have already started adopting a few. This guide is a playbook for long-term, lasting development.

It is our very human inclination to try to stamp out uncertainty—and of course, we should try to make the world as predictable as we can. Because you are choosing to read this book, I'm betting that you, like thousands of other leaders, realize (or suspect) that stamping out uncertainty is impossible and are ready to rethink conventional approaches. I'm excited to share with you what I've discovered, to set the stage for a new way of thinking, to open eyes, fill your cup with ideas, and engage your curiosity in such a way that you will be motivated to take your marketing management in a more fruitful direction.

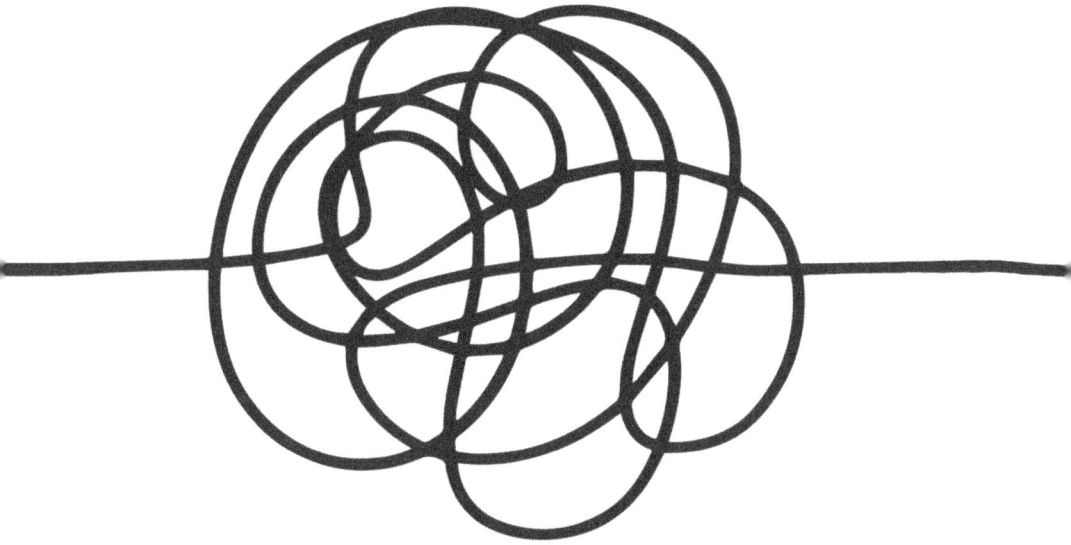

PART I

WHERE WE ARE, HOW WE GOT THERE, AND WHERE WE NEED TO GO

There are two chapters in the initial section of this book. The first chapter explores the origins of the misalignment between marketing's complex nature and traditional management paradigms and how, with the help of science, people figured out what went wrong. That chapter will help you understand why a new approach to marketing leadership and operations is needed. The second chapter reveals the amazing backdrop for the remedy. Together, these stories prepare you with the information needed to convince others about the need for change. Here is a quick preview of these chapters:

- **Why the Quest for Predictable Marketing Is Doomed:** The industrial era manufactured a management philosophy that business, including marketing, could be run like a machine. Companies labored to achieve deterministic efficiency, and while progress was made, you'll learn why this approach was doomed from the outset when applied to anything related to people or nature. Yet, this old style is still incredibly common today.

- **Different Thinking, Different Actions: Creating Conditions for Marketing Success:** Fortunately, new approaches that are purpose-built for variable and unpredictable environments have emerged and are gaining traction. You'll discover the foundations for the mindsets and capabilities required for marketing success in this complex digital era.

CHAPTER 1

WHY THE QUEST FOR PREDICTABLE MARKETING IS DOOMED

The demand for certainty is one which is natural to man but is nevertheless an intellectual vice.

—**Bertrand Russell,** *Unpopular Essays*

L ife is full of the unexpected: This is something we all accept. Some surprises are delightful. A random conversation at a party opens the door to your dream job. You find twenty bucks in the pocket of a coat you haven't worn for years. A free upgrade is offered to you for a long flight. Some surprises are less delightful. You are driving at the speed limit when traffic suddenly increases, blocking the freeway for hours. Plans for an outdoor wedding get foiled by an unexpected downpour. A tiny bat virus escapes its host and unleashes a pandemic.

Not everything in life is uncertain, of course. The laws of physics, such as thermodynamics, apply always and everywhere. Math is consistent. Two plus two will equal four every day for thousands of years. But whenever nature enters the picture, especially living things who enjoy independent agency, an X factor gets introduced that makes situations unpredictable. And given that marketing's realm is composed of people who are perhaps the most unpredictable force in nature, it's not surprising that marketing must learn to deal with that X factor in spades. In this chapter, I provide some historical perspective on how industrial-era leaders confronted unpredictability in business and marketing. I also explain why their approach—although widely used and extremely successful in some arenas—fails in marketing because marketing's very nature is resistant to certainty.

THE QUEST FOR MACHINE-LIKE CONTROL

Since time immemorial, people have tried to clarify the uncertain future and wrestle it into submission. For business management, possibly no one did more for that effort than Frederick Winslow Taylor, whose book *The Principles of Scientific Management*, first published in 1911, became the best-selling business book in the first half of the twentieth century. Business guru Peter Drucker later called it "the most powerful as well as the most lasting contribution that America has made to Western thought since the Federalist Papers."[1] The book is still in print.

Taylor's innovation derived from his conviction that the same scientific rigor that made machines better could make work processes more efficient and outcomes more predictable. When Taylor began his career in a Pennsylvania steel mill, machinists functioned like artisan guild members, a style of work that had dominated production for hundreds of years. Work was a craft. Knowledge was held tight by experienced workers. Rules of thumb, tips and tricks, and trade secrets passed to apprentices only after years of commitment. Precise measurement was nonexistent. This work style resulted in significant variability in quality, time, and cost. When Taylor asked why a worker hammered a certain shape or selected a particular tool, he got shrugs. Every worker applied a personalized art to his job.

Taylor set out on a course to discover what became known as "the one best way" to do everything. Armed with a stopwatch and slide rule, Taylor applied the tools of classical mechanics to the steel mills where he was employed. He deconstructed tasks into granular elements, each of which was studied, experimented with, improved, and reconstructed. He took intricate measurements of everything. Nothing was too insignificant. He redesigned shovels to increase the load of coal delivery to furnaces. He determined the best motions for laying bricks, identified the exact right temperature to cool lathes, and the perfect speed for conveyor belts. Taylor called his new approach *scientific management*, and its benefits were astounding. At the 1900 Paris Exposition, Taylor demonstrated how by simply changing the way people worked, a steel mill could increase the amount of steel cut per minute by over 500 percent.

Once the gains from Taylor's machine-oriented work system were publicized, scientific management spread like wildfire. The core structure of American schools, including grade levels and standardized testing, were inspired by scientific management. White collar workers learned how to clip papers in the "one best way." Government and churches seized on Taylor's methods. One of Taylor's students, Henry Gantt, invented the field of modern project management.

Scientific management was also a perfect match for the military. America's success in the two World Wars relied heavily on scientific management approaches. Taylorism converted tens of thousands of untrained sharecroppers and housewives into soldiers and shipbuilders in a flash. The unprecedented production of weapons and equipment would not have been possible without Taylor's methods.

The explosive success of industrial production required businesses to rethink their commercial capability. Mass production required mass marketing and mass distribution. To accomplish this objective, leaders again sought advice from the now acclaimed field of scientific management. As tiny companies gave way to manufacturers aspiring to become national—even international—brands, marketers began to seek ways to scale and professionalize their discipline.

Percival White, a pioneer in market research, linked the work of Taylor into actionable directions for commercial marketing. White was a prolific contributor to his emerging field, writing well-received books such as *Scientific Marketing Management: Its Principles and Methods* and *Market Analysis*. In 1932, the American Marketing Society (later the American Marketing Association or AMA) was founded, specifically dedicated to the science of marketing.

CRACKS IN THE MACHINE MODEL

Taylorism was a practical solution to the real problems of the first half of the twentieth century, and it was able to rid organizations of much chaos and waste. For decades, companies using this model outperformed. But even as scientific management flourished, it became increasingly apparent that the further work strayed from repetitious, limited-skill labor, the harder it became to find the "one best way," and the more that environments diverged from the sphere of the industrial shop floor, the less measurable and less predictable things became.

One area of concern was the injurious effects of Taylorism on workers. Some steel workers would be unable to get out of bed the day after a shift in a Taylor-driven mill. The people challenge deepened as automation devoured many of the manual jobs that Taylorism had made efficient, and the number of knowledge workers increased.[2] By mid-century, the number of knowledge workers surpassed manual workers. By the 1960s, management theorists were aggressively denouncing scientific management's perspective that workers were components in the machine of labor. MIT Professor Douglas McGregor's "Theory X and Theory Y" approach asserted that humans were capable of much more than being mere widgets and deserved respect. It may be astounding to today's managers that basic respect for human workers needed to be called out, yet these theories were revolutionary at the time.

DISCOVERY OF COMPLEXITY AND THE BUTTERFLY EFFECT

Working conditions were not the only sphere where applying the principles of the machine metaphor experienced mixed outcomes. Nature also didn't fall in line. On one hand, the industrial-era obsession for scientifically dissecting, analyzing, categorizing, and improving nature led to dramatic improvements in food supply and health outcomes. But in other ways, nature continued to confound scientists. Examples of the unintended consequences resulting from people trying to reduce nature to a controllable machine were common.

Particularly painful are stories about the introduction of invasive species. One example: In the 1930s, Australia imported 102 Hawaiian cane toads to rid sugarcane fields of voracious greyback beetle grubs. The toad population now covers 40 percent of Queensland. Their expansion was fostered by the absence of Hawaiian predators, the abundance of food-filled ponds, and the gross underestimation of toad fertility. The toad species eats almost anything—except greyback beetle grubs. Differences in life cycles between Hawaii and Australia mean toads and beetles are never in the field at the same time.[3]

With the arrival of data-crunching computers, scientists began to discover why the machine model regularly failed in nature. Edward Lorenz, an assistant professor at MIT, made an astounding revelation while trying to figure out how to predict the weather. Working as a weather forecaster for the US Army Air Corp during World War II had sparked a passion in the young mathematician, and he pursued a doctorate with the exciting prospect of applying the power of emerging computer technology to climate prediction. No longer would farmers, pilots, and picnickers muddle through by simply watching the sky.

By 1961, Lorenz was eight years into a frustratingly slow project running computer simulations analyzing variables such as temperature and wind speed. Despite much effort, no significant progress had been made in weather predictability. One day, when repeating yet one more simulation, he took a shortcut. Using results from a printout run the day before, Lorenz started a simulation midway through. Computers were slow in 1961, so he went for coffee while the program ran, fully expecting that the second simulation results would duplicate those of the first. Upon his return, Lorenz was shocked and confused to discover that the results of the two programs diverged wildly! What happened?

After weeks of investigation, Lorenz tracked down the reason. The data used in the two simulations were *not* identical as he had intended. The computer's memory stored value out to six decimal points. However, the printout that Lorenz had used as a reference recorded only three. If weather was regular and deterministic, like a machine, any difference between the two simulations should have been inconsequential. Instead, Lorenz realized that just the tiny rounding error had caused the two simulations to career in irrationally different directions.

What Lorenz had discovered was *non-linearity*, a fundamental principle of what became known as *chaos theory* and later was incorporated into *complexity science*. His discovery meant that, sadly, the world would never be able to precisely predict long-term weather. Non-linearity is a fundamental characteristic of complex systems. Weather is a complex system formed from the tangled connectivity of billions of factors, including temperature, geography, and wind speed. Non-linearity implies that because of those interactions, a small change in the initial state of a process often causes monumental change later. People nicknamed Lorenz's discovery the *butterfly effect* from the poetic example Lorenz used for the title of his 1972 talk, "Does the Flap of a Butterfly's Wings in Brazil Set off a Tornado in Texas?"

BUTTERFLIES AND MARKETING: IT'S A VUCA WORLD

Marketing's ever-changing character emanates from its reality as what scientists call a *complex system*. Interactions between individuals, buying groups, and enterprises, each of whom is a singular blend of motivations, preferences, desires, and behaviors, create feedback loops producing many unknowns and uncertain outcomes. The more entities who interact, the more amplified complexity's effects. This condition is captured by the acronym VUCA:

- **Volatile,** meaning there is a high rate and variability of change. Amplified variability produces more extreme tumult.

- **Uncertain,** meaning there is a lack of clarity about the future. A high degree of rapid change means more unknowns and thus increased risk.

- **Complex,** indicating not only extremely complicated situations but the strange and unique attributes of complex systems that science had begun to identify.

- **Ambiguous** conveys how situations and outcomes can have multiple interpretations.

Volatile. Uncertain. Complex. Ambiguous. VUCA. Anyone who has practiced marketing even for a short time knows in their heart of hearts that marketing is VUCA, in large part because of the unpredictability of human interactions. VUCA is a word and concept I use throughout this book, so allow me to provide a little more background on what it means.

The acronym has its roots in military theaters, which have always been chaotic. Following the Cold War, the US Army found they were facing an even more complex world that produced very different circumstances than the conflicts they had earlier prepared for. Gone were planned battles between regimented armies and formidable equipment. Gone were situations that generals could command and control. Instead, soldiers embedded in cities teeming with frightened citizens. They faced conflicts with opportunistic, fast-moving enemies. It is from facing this puzzle that the term VUCA[4] emerged. Drawing on the leadership theories of Warren Bennis and Burt Nanus, the US Army War College adopted the term in the 1990s to describe these conditions and introduced the concept into their leadership training. Since that time, the VUCA term has spread into many sectors.

Prussian field marshal Helmuth von Moltke famously stated in the late nineteenth century that "no plan survives first contact with the enemy."[5] The VUCA marketplace means that no marketing plan survives first contact

Figure 1.1: Complexity arises wherever independent agents interact with each other and their environment.

Source: Kathleen Schaub 2023

with customers. The path between strategic plans and revenue realization is not a straight road but rather a waterway of rivers and streams that could go almost anywhere. Marketing and sales teams—operating at the tumultuous edge where the company meets its customers—encounter dozens, hundreds, maybe millions of VUCA interactions daily, so it's easy to understand why the environment seems chaotic. VUCA conditions are why customer journeys are more like a child's scribble than an orderly funnel. VUCA is why an ad campaign can bump along for weeks and then suddenly take off or fail. VUCA is why salespeople find marketing leads disappointing, and marketing's VUCA reality is also what dooms the quest for predictable marketing ROI.[6]

All natural and social environments are VUCA. People who work in healthcare, first response teams, gaming, software development, environmental ecosystems, and stock markets, as well as the military, are among the many workers with challenges similar to marketers. (See figure 1.1.) While it's rare that what happens in marketing carries the weighty consequences of military theaters, both situations have a common challenge—you never know what's going to happen next.

HOW THE MODERN WORLD INCREASES VUCA EFFECTS

While the marketplace has always been VUCA, the modern world has amplified and accelerated complexity's effects. The highly interconnected world means that twenty-first century businesses encounter complexity and its VUCA characteristics with greater frequency and often with greater consequences, affecting marketing in the following ways.

Accelerated Interactions Due to Digital Technology

Digital technology increases complexity by escalating connectedness, which in turn generates more interactions and accelerates the pace of those interactions. People, events, things, and places that were previously more isolated or far away are now virtually adjacent. Messages fire instantly from person to person and system to system. Feedback is instantaneous. Everything is constantly in our faces. Removing the traditional constraints of distance, scale, intelligence, and malleability has caused an explosion of innovation and disruption. What worked five minutes ago may not work now, so requirements are constantly shifting. The differences that today's digital world imposes on work are summarized in figure 1.2.

Industrial-Era World:	Today's Digital World:
1. Requirements are known ahead of time	1. Requirements are **uncertain**
2. Requirements are stable	2. Requirements **constantly change**
3. Long time between planning and delivery	3. Need **speed** between **sense and respond**
4. Required outcomes are repeatable	4. Required outcomes are **highly variable**
5. Production requires low-skilled workers	5. Production requires **highly skilled workers**

Figure 1.2: Comparison of Work Requirements, Industrial vs. Digital Worlds

Source: Kathleen Schaub 2021

To manage this surge, marketing is forced to speed up and adapt. Before the digital transformation, there were fewer channels, buyers had fewer choices, and vendors had fewer competitors. In slower times, marketers had time to think, to prepare, and react. As digital accelerated interactions, word of mouth spread more quickly. Now, the luxury of time has all but disappeared, increasing the risk of inappropriate knee-jerk responses, wasted churn, lost opportunity, and poor decisions. Skilled marketers have lost the breathing space needed to work through situational ambiguities.

Increased Business Model Transformation

The continuous introduction of new technologies and new business models results in old ones being commoditized or replaced. The result has been a big turnover in companies. McKinsey reports that only 10 percent of the 1983 nonfinancial companies on the S&P 500 list were still there in 2013.[7] Ecommerce, online health, and online education are just a few core services that are dramatically different from just a decade ago. Physical industries are changing too. Tesla's rethinking of supply chains, for example, contributed to them leaving other electric vehicle manufacturers in the dust.[8] Peer-to-peer services such as Uber, Airbnb, and PayPal have disrupted a range of industries. The expansion of artificial intelligence promises to disrupt at perhaps an even bigger scale.

To thrive, innovation is required, not just for products and services but also for the methods of doing business, including in marketing. New business models call for marketing methods to adapt.

Rising Customer Power

The increased volume, transparency, availability, and multidirectional spreading of information tilted market power in favor of customers. Customers have more choices. It is easier than ever to switch products, services, and suppliers. Product features and price matter but are more quickly copied. Digital services enable companies to lower costs and make product trial, purchase, and use easier. Customers gang up, disseminating opinions and experiences (frequently negative) about company reputation. Today, companies can rarely gain competitive advantage without excellent customer experience. Engaged customers are more likely to purchase, to recommend, and to be loyal. Combined with global competition and increasingly consumer-friendly regulations, no company can take customer loyalty for granted.

Rising Employee Power

Throughout history, technology has automated jobs that used to be done by humans. Humans adapt over time, employing their time and energy in other work requiring higher-level or different skills. During the period of adaptation, there are always fewer workers with these skills available, and the shortage increases employee power. Skilled employees get choosier and can make more demands. To attract the best workers, companies must offer more value than their competitors. For example, today's companies must adapt work environments and offer perks and purpose beyond a paycheck if they want to attract the best talent to help them be productive.

Changing Sources of Value

Companies generated value in the industrial era by mastering production, often by creating economies of scale and repetition. Improving efficiency in established processes, while it remains important in the sense that too much inefficiency makes a company uncompetitive, offers little differentiation because in most cases, everyone uses the same technologies. Rarely in today's world can a business profit by providing the same thing to every customer. Instead, value comes from innovation and from tailoring products and services. This requires the ability to manage a kaleidoscope of changing requirements and respond to opportunities that pop up. Companies succeed by excelling in inventiveness, creativity, problem-solving, and relationships—all of which are traits that humans excel at.

FIVE WAYS THAT MARKETING RESISTS MACHINE-LIKE PREDICTABILITY

While modern management techniques evolved as a way to improve predictability, the VUCA nature of the marketplace guarantees that this is an impossible goal for marketing. Here are five specific ways that unpredictability is an inevitable condition for marketing.

1. Markets Are Composed of Multiple Heterogeneous, Interdependent Agents

All machines have parts; most of them contain a large number of parts. But these parts are limited and purpose-built, and no component acts independently. Markets, on the other hand, are tangled by the interactions of autonomous (self-directing) individuals (e.g., buyers, entrepreneurs, salespeople, marketers, influencers); groups (e.g., buying groups, teams, clubs); and enterprises (e.g., corporations, media companies, regulatory agencies, supply chain participants). Each of these agents can and does act independently of all other agents. They adapt their behavior according to local motivation, context, and exposure to information and environmental signals.

2. Control Is Distributed; No One Is in Charge

People control machines, and outcomes can be specified. Executives typically believe (or wish) that marketers are the "mission control" of their campaigns. But market behavior isn't governed by any controller, so marketers can only intervene and influence. Active agents in complex systems react and adapt to their environment rather than being directed top down. This distributed control makes marketing more like raising a child than building a car: There is no one-size-fits-all best practice or checklist.

3. Markets Are, at Best, Semi-Predictable

A machine's performance can be replicated because the same starting conditions produce the same outcomes. Tap lightly on the accelerator and the car inches forward, or press the pedal to the metal to make the car race. In contrast, the non-linearity (the butterfly effect) of complex systems means continual surprises. Small changes, especially early, can have profound effects later. A brief chance encounter at a conference in 2024 can lead to a huge deal in 2027. Alternatively, large actions may have little or no effect, as when sales decrease despite a large ad buy. Markets have patterns, which makes them at least semi-predictable, and anything predictable can be modeled, though that predictability is limited by the bounds of time and probability (the likelihood that something will happen).

4. Market-Level Behavior Patterns Emerge from the Swarm of Participant Interactions

Machine performance is predictable if you know how machine components work. Machines are logical and reductive, and what happens at a macro level is directly caused by adding up all the component actions. The behavior of complex systems, in contrast, comes about in an entirely different way. Complex systems have this weird, almost magical propensity called *emergence* that means they can form higher-level patterns on their own. That is, patterns of behavior can arise that are not directly related to the behavior of any individual and without anyone trying to exert control. Traffic is a good example of an emergent phenomena. Traffic behavior, such as jams, arises from the interactions of cars, drivers, and the environment and can't be predicted by understanding the behavior of any single driver.

Understanding the concept of emergence is critical for knowing the boundaries of what can and cannot be predicted when it comes to marketing effectiveness and ROI. Emergence is a tremendously powerful phenomenon. You'll encounter this concept throughout the book.

5. Measuring Marketing ROI Is Challenging Because of Blurred Boundaries

A main genesis of this book was the perplexing demand by C-suite executives for predictable, easily measured ROI from marketing efforts. That task is impossible not just because of the unpredictability of marketing but because measuring ROI from marketing efforts is a challenge unto itself.

One of the biggest marketing ROI challenges stems from a lack of a consistent definition of what's in the ROI calculation. Calculating ROI requires distinct category boundaries. Every machine component is distinct. But nothing about a market is distinct, and this causes organizations to disagree about the artificial perimeters that marketers must impose to attempt to figure out ROI. The 2018 Proof Analytics study revealed that 95 percent of executive respondents weren't sure marketing leaders had the same understanding of value creation as business leaders.[9] More likely, even the business leaders who responded to this survey would not agree with each other! Areas of contention include:

- What does "return" mean? Does return refer only to financial outcomes or should important benefits such as customer loyalty or company reputation be included?

- Where should measurement start and stop? Given the time lag between marketing actions and outcomes, how much historical data should be taken into consideration?

- How should the ripple effects of marketing actions be treated? For example, should revenue from referrals be included in the ROI calculation?

PREDICTABILITY IS DOOMED

Modern management philosophies and models all have their roots in the search for predictability, reliability, and precision launched by Frederick Taylor a century ago. When it comes to marketing, management has not yet fully adapted to what is now recognized to be a VUCA world. That VUCA-ness and the associated five conditions just discussed—multiple, independent agents; distributed control; only semi-predictable; emergent behavior; and blurred boundaries—make it clear that the quest for a high degree of marketing predictability is doomed.

While devotion to efficiency brought tremendous benefits to many sectors of the economy and its practices are deeply embedded in business culture, the complex reality of marketing defies machine-like operations. The interconnection of individuals, groups, and enterprises, combined with environmental influences, means that markets will always generate non-linearity and emergent behavior. It doesn't matter how much executives would like marketing to operate like a machine; it's never going to happen, regardless of the best management, exemplary intentions, abundant data, excellent tools, perfect processes, or intense effort. And we've learned that the overapplication of machine approaches can have disastrous results. The option to continue trying to beat marketing into a predictable machine will only result in continuing frustration and disappointment.

There is another way. As the poet Robert Frost once wrote, "The best way out is always through."[10] Leaders can embrace the market's true nature and learn the new mindsets and methods better suited for succeeding in a living system.

TAKE THIS AWAY

Executives have long tried to treat marketing like a machine, expecting predictable outcomes to result from controlled inputs. But marketing is about people, and everything related to the way humans behave and interact generates complex systems, where inputs and outputs seldom correlate. Leaders need to recognize that marketing is inherently unpredictable.

Key takeaways from this chapter include the following:

- **Common marketing management practices are largely based on industrial-era assumptions.** Many practices emerged from the work of Frederick Winslow Taylor's scientific management philosophy, which attempted to apply machine-like rigor to labor. While this movement produced many positives, Tayloresque approaches have always been problematic for marketing.

- **Marketing is best characterized as a "complex system,"** the same as all other natural and social systems. Interactions between individuals, buying groups, and enterprises—each of which is a singular blend of motivations, preferences, desires, and behaviors— produce many unknowns and uncertain outcomes.

- **The characteristics of complex systems are true for marketing.** These include **non-linearity (the butterfly effect)** and **emergence** (the appearance of unpredictable patterns that result from the combination of individual actors in the system but cannot be traced to any single source).

- **Marketing's world is VUCA** (volatile, uncertain, complex, and ambiguous). VUCA is the term often used to characterize the conditions encountered in marketing. Awareness of the VUCA nature of marketing has a major impact on leadership decisions and expectations. The speed of communication and change in the modern world is increasing the VUCA nature of the marketing environment.

- **Because of its VUCA nature, a high degree of predictability in marketing is doomed.** To thrive, managers must embrace marketing's complexity and adopt more useful mindsets and methods.

CHAPTER 2

DIFFERENT THINKING, DIFFERENT ACTIONS: CREATING CONDITIONS FOR MARKETING SUCCESS

If we cannot control the volatile tides of change,
we can learn to build better boats.

—**Andrew Zolli,** *Resilience: Why Things Bounce Back*

One of my prized possessions is a crystal vase that was given to me by a sales rep. I received it as a thank-you from Mike, one of my company's best account managers, for helping him win a landmark contract with a significant client. Long before the term account-based marketing (ABM) became famous, marketers would sometimes work side-by-side with a sales team, participating in win-room strategy planning, creating customer-specific content and other customized work.

In this instance, Mike and I had arrived late in the afternoon in the snowy northern city of the prospective client's headquarters, ready to pitch our technology-infused transformation service the next morning. But when Mike checked in with his main contact, he got a big surprise. A new, very skeptical executive had joined the buying group and would have a lot of questions for us, questions that we had not prepared for in our current presentation.

If we wanted to win this project, Mike and I had little choice but to rework the message. So, we trudged to an all-night business center where we labored until 2 a.m. Our adapted presentation was successful, and we won the contract. After the meeting, we debriefed with the client employee who was Mike's connection. The client explained that, unbeknownst to us, the new executive had earlier conducted independent research on our company and had talked to others, inside and outside the company, in preparation for grilling us. Fortunately, what the executive had learned enhanced our chances of a positive outcome.

What Mike and I experienced is another example of how customer engagements can take unexpected turns. The way we responded to the altered circumstances illustrates one of the foundations required to thrive in marketing's VUCA world. We demonstrated *agility*. We sought intelligence and then collaborated to nimbly and quickly adapt to the changed situational context. Although agility was necessary, it was not sufficient to win the deal. Fortunately, our company had invested in what I call *market system health*, actions which develop the conditions—both inside the company and out in the market—that improved our chances of succeeding despite all the twists and turns of the customer journey.

In this chapter, I talk more about agility and market system health and how they relate to what is required for marketing to thrive in a VUCA world. I then provide an overview of the shifts in thinking and operational practices required to make those objectives a reality. These mind shifts and capabilities are the subject of parts II and III, respectively.

WHY AGILITY IS ESSENTIAL

Unexpected things constantly pop up in marketing. Sometimes the surprise will be negative ("Oh no, a competitor just introduced a better product than ours!"), other times favorable ("The current news cycle just produced a tailwind that amplified our campaign!"), or they may just offer a pivotal juncture where things could go either way, as it did for Mike and me. In any case, you will be better off if you can optimally respond. Greater agility can be developed with the appropriate ways of thinking and acting. The chapters in part II of this book, Embracing Complexity, and part III, Engaging Complexity, describe shifts that will boost marketing's agility.

To some people, the term *agility* may suggest the specific practices of the Agile methodologies (spelled with a capital "A") that are common in software development, IT, and increasingly adopted in marketing organizations. These Agile methodologies are purpose-built for uncertainty and, therefore, help companies thrive in a VUCA world. Some Agile Marketing practices are discussed further in chapter 9: The Work Method: An Agile Operation. However, the agility (small "a") essential for responsiveness in VUCA markets isn't limited to these formal methods.

Agility, at a higher level, means the power to change ideas, attitudes, actions, and behavior flexibly and quickly in response to new situations, conditions, environments, or purposes. Agility provides these advantages:

- Enables *opportunism* (the ability to take advantage of potential benefits as they unexpectedly arise)

- Supports *resilience* (the ability to avoid, withstand, or bounce back after hardship or disruption)

- Increases *innovation* (the ability to design new strategies for new conditions)

- Assists in developing *equanimity* (the ability to flourish psychologically and emotionally under a variety of conditions)

The VUCA nature of complex systems isn't limited to marketing, and agility is beneficial in many areas of company operations (supply chain, security, product development, and information technology are a few examples). CEOs understand this. In a 2021 study conducted by the IBM Institute for Business Value,[1] 56 percent of CEOs emphasized the need to "aggressively pursue" operational agility over the next 2–3 years, and this task ranked highest among the top 3 priorities of total respondents. Companies will miss out on a tremendous opportunity if they don't also extend agility to marketing.

FOCUS ON MARKET SYSTEM HEALTH TO PROMOTE SUCCESS

The story of Mike's and my client presentation had a happy ending because the company we worked for had set the stage for victory. Not all the helpful preconditions were related to marketing, but many were. For instance, our company had built a trusted brand that originally inspired the client to consider our service, we had a well-organized website that contained thoughtful content, and our articles in important media sources answered the new executive's questions and overcame his concerns. Years of developing influence and positive customer experiences ensured vital recommendations, and the education and training that prepared Mike and me for our work that night made the sale possible. No one could have known ahead of time which elements would be needed in this exact situation. We could have predicted with some probability which pieces of content would be viewed but not known for sure, and we couldn't be certain which company clients would be called on for referrals. But by ensuring that a sufficient foundation was in place for all these things and more, we increased our chances of a win, and it worked.

That's the core of what I call market system health: If you properly prepare all the parts of your marketing system, you can be more confident that any changes in the market will work in your favor.

To some people, the concept of market system health will call to mind the term *brand health*. Brand, which refers to the distinctive characteristics that identify an enterprise, product, or person, is certainly a major contributor to overall market system health. However, market system health is broader in meaning than brand. By comparison, think about human biological health, which encompasses physical, mental, and social well-being. Developing and maintaining biological health requires generative habits—ones that "generate" optimal body conditions. Generative habits include eating nutritional food, participating in regular exercise, getting sufficient sleep, and connecting regularly with family and friends. Together, these build strong, resilient bodies and minds that help a person accomplish their goals and resist and recover from disease.

Market system health is similarly broad. To build a company's healthy foundation in a market, enterprises must also practice long-term generative habits. Within this book, I identify elements that will promote the development of a healthy marketing system, including how to think about marketing as a system and how to make operational changes that will move your company toward improved market system health.

The journey to essential market system health starts with holistic thinking, which considers everything in relation to everything else. American naturalist John Muir wrote, "When we try to pick out anything by itself, we find it hitched to everything else in the Universe."[2] This is the connectivity of systems thinking. A system is a set of things—people, forests, cells, molecules, or whatever—interconnected in such a way that they produce their own patterns of behavior over time,[3] according to Donella H. Meadows, author of *Thinking in Systems: A Primer*. If you pull a string in a system, the effects reverberate through space and time. A change made in one area of a system—even if it is minor like a butterfly flapping its wings or a message served to a customer at the right moment—produces changes in ways you often can't see.

In fact, most of a system is hidden from view yet will be working under the surface—often with power. A common metaphor for a system is an iceberg. While only perhaps 10 percent of the iceberg may be seen above the ocean surface, the hidden 90 percent influences the ocean and the iceberg's behavior.[4] The events that any one person can observe in the world, like the visible 10 percent of the iceberg, represents only a small portion of what is happening or has happened in the system. You can't know when your immune system is going to need that bit of vitamin C from the strawberry you just ate, but at any moment it could. You can't know when an unidentified power buyer will go searching for that obscure bit of content about your service practices, but at some moment they could—and it could make or break a purchase decision.

Each of us experiences our corner of the world through our personal window of space and time. What we personally observe is a tiny manifestation emerging from an immense, dynamic, interconnected network of unobserved activity. Some activity hidden from an individual may be experienced by other humans or by our intelligent machines, and we can broaden our perspective by pooling perceptions, but most of the bustling system will remain forever in shadow.

The same phenomenon is true of marketing. Markets, which are made of people, are part of nature and therefore best represented by systems thinking. This is the opposite of reductive machine thinking, which cuts the world into pieces and spreads them apart. It is that connectivity of the parts of the system that produces VUCA. And it is the unknown, hidden parts of the marketing iceberg that make marketing resistant to prediction. Yet, it is also that connectivity that gives systems amazing power.

PROGRESS STARTS BY EMBRACING NEW MINDSETS

Mindsets govern attitudes, actions, and orientation, regardless of how aware we are of our beliefs. Conscious or unconscious, mindsets have far-reaching influence. They direct actions, which in turn produce consequences. Buddhism provides a useful analogy: The oxen pulling a cart determines the cartwheel's path. The oxen are like our views and intentions, the cartwheels like our behaviors and actions. The cart cannot go anywhere the oxen doesn't lead it.

Mental models developed from a machine-oriented culture are oxen that can take you only in directions you've already gone. If they deploy traditional mindsets, enterprises will continue to reinforce ineffective structures and actions that contribute to marketing's persistent challenges. We must change the direction of the oxen before there is a chance of getting the cart to a new place. Following even a slight bend in the path will, over the long haul, take us miles from where we might have gone otherwise.

Viewing marketing through a different prism offers extraordinary power because it shines light on new possibilities. Different analogies, new language, and reframing become the emotional intelligence tools that provoke us into questioning the beliefs and practices that keep things locked in the status quo.

Mind shifts in key areas of a marketing leader's responsibility will generate the greatest power. Specifically, executives must think differently about these responsibilities:

1. How they manage resources
2. How they plan and measure
3. How they make decisions
4. How they manage their people

The four chapters in part II contain insights from other professions that have learned to effectively deal with turbulence. These insights can help marketing leaders and practitioners better understand how marketing really works and why certain practices are more effective than others under VUCA conditions. Table 2.A summarizes these guiding mind shifts and lists the chapters where you can find more details.

Responsibility	Old Mindset	New Mindset
Manage resources	Marketing is a cost center	Marketing is an investment (*See chapter 3: Think Like an Investor*)
Planning and measurement	Keeping score against advanced plans	Adaptively navigating through marketing's shifting context (*See chapter 4: Think Like a Navigator*)
Decision-making	Seek certainty	Accept and work with probabilities (*See chapter 5: Think Like a Statistician*)
People management	Focus primarily on top-down directives and individual's success	Create an environment where people can thrive (*See chapter 6: Think Like an Ecologist*)

Table 2.A: Shifts in Mindsets Required for Leadership in an Uncertain World

As part of the concepts included in the mind shift chapters, I highlight several cognitive biases that can become barriers to adopting new mindsets, and it's useful to be aware of these. Cognitive biases, as defined by Encyclopedia Britannica, are predictable patterns of errors in how human brains function.[5] Biased thinking occurs when thinking travels in a predictable—but faulty—direction. Think of an archer whose arrows consistently land just a little up and to the left of the target center.

Humans evolved biases to make fast choices under ambiguous conditions. Survival once depended on a speedy reaction to a rustle in the savannah grass. We might be wrong, but at least we stayed alive. While we no longer risk a lion's assault, modern life throws plenty of surprises in our path. No matter how hard we prepare, we always have insufficient knowledge and processing capability to handle life in the messy world.

Biases evolved to help us stay alive, but they can also work against our best intentions. Within the mind shift chapters, I call out a few of the riskiest biases related to that mind shift. To start with, one of the most powerful and risky biases is the *blind spot bias*, which drives us to recognize biases in other peoples' thinking but makes us fail to see them in ourselves. When under the sway of the blind spot bias, you feel that you are less biased than the average person. Undoubtably at some point, everyone reading about mental biases will think, "Glad that's not me!" As you read about the various mind shifts, it's helpful to stay aware of this universal tendency rather than assume that this situation doesn't apply to you.

NEW MINDSETS SIGNAL IMPORTANT OPERATIONAL SHIFTS

Mindsets are the oxen that pull the cart of actions, but it is the actions that produce consequences. Oprah Winfrey once quoted Maya Angelou as saying, "You did what you knew how to do, and when you knew better, you did better."[6] ComplexityWise mind shifts will help leaders know better, and developing ComplexityWise capabilities will help them do better. In operations as with mind shifts, where scientific management instructed leaders to dismantle and compartmentalize, systems knowledge guides us to leverage the power of connection.

As with mindsets, the shifts in certain operational capabilities carry extra power for succeeding in marketing's VUCA reality. The chapters in part III present to marketing leaders the practical guidance about operational shifts needed in the following capabilities:

- **Information processes:** Intelligence is incredibly fundamental to agility and to the optimal development of market system health. Upgrading and integrating technical systems (including artificial intelligence) with human contributions is essential. (See chapter 7: The Information System: Collective Intelligence.)

- **Organizational structures:** Moving away from traditional silos and lofty hierarchies to more flexible and connected organizational structures improves the ability to boost customer experience and offers benefits to employees. (See chapter 8: The Organization: Integrated Teams.)

- **Work methods:** Possibly the most mature of the capability shifts needed for ComplexityWise marketing are the optimal work processes that leverage Agile methods. When balanced with selected practices from the industrial era, these provide more flexible ways of navigating changing context. (See chapter 9: The Work Method: An Agile Operation.)

- **Transformation:** While change is always a challenge, the connectivity of systems offers the strange characteristic of emergence as an underutilized and almost magical power to make things move. (See chapter 10: The Change Management Method: Leverage Emergence.)

Within each capability chapter, I describe specific practices that enable your organization to get beneficial outcomes even though you're operating in a VUCA environment. As with any new practice, you can expect results to start appearing after a moderate stretch of implementation. They improve with continuous effort, and each beneficial practice helps you improve the others. The chapter on emergent transformation is an important companion to every effort to develop ComplexityWise marketing. These practices help leaders better understand how change works in a system and why some expectations for quick fixes typically don't work.

When developing ComplexityWise capabilities, the objective is not to completely abandon everything learned from the past. In fact, some situations merit pushing selected aspects of the machine model even further. For instance, breaking down big monolithic projects into smaller parts (called *reductionism* in Taylor's scientific management) can improve flexibility. ComplexityWise marketing capabilities are best thought of as containing the "yes, and" stance of improv theater. These practices seek to rebalance where machine-oriented approaches have gone too far. The choice that industrial-era managers faced between chaos and inefficiency or rigid, centralized standardization has become a false one. We now have methods and technologies that were unknown or unavailable to earlier generations to get the best of both worlds.

COMPLEXITYWISE SKILLS REQUIRED FOR CMOS

What you may infer from the discussion in this chapter—and will certainly confront in later chapters—is that the adoption of ComplexityWise marketing requires CMOs to strengthen certain skills of their own. You will find, for example, that some practices I recommend require executive support and collaboration from beyond the marketing department. Certainly, CMOs can make progress while working solely within the departmental silo walls to which the traditional corporation confines them. However, more can be accomplished with cross-functional partnerships because every customer journey bounces among various company functions and solutions often need skills and assistance from many areas. This need for cooperation requires CMOs and other marketing leaders to cultivate such skills as communicating vision, creating connections, and facilitating change. Throughout this book, you will find ideas and insight for these and other competencies that will be especially valuable in complex environments.

TAKE THIS AWAY

The objectives of agility and market system health can never be achieved if we continue to think and act in ways that are mired in the machine perspective of the industrial era.

To be successful in marketing's VUCA reality requires ComplexityWise marketing, the mindsets and capability practices that increase agility, thus boosting your ability to optimally respond to whatever pops up and improve market system health, which increases the chances that whatever uncontrollable things happen in the market will occur in your favor (see figure 2.1). ComplexityWise marketing works by activating the human potential for problem-solving while leveraging technology to augment human capabilities.

COMPLEXITYWISE MARKETING

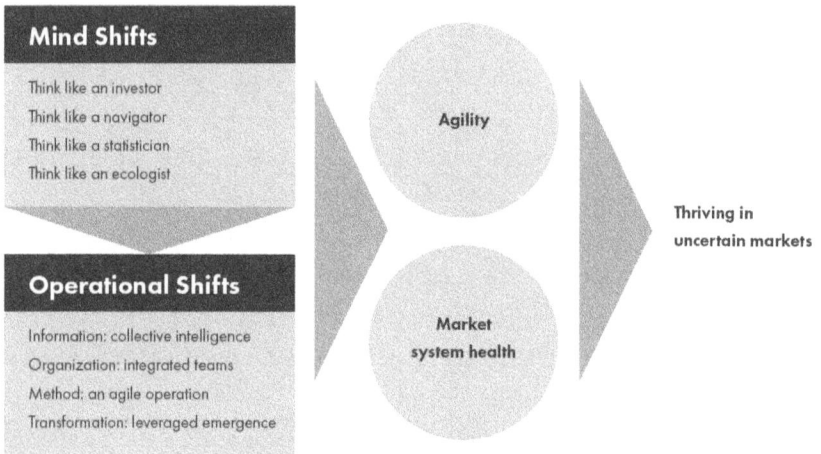

Mind Shifts
Think like an investor
Think like a navigator
Think like a statistician
Think like an ecologist

Operational Shifts
Information: collective intelligence
Organization: integrated teams
Method: an agile operation
Transformation: leveraged emergence

Agility

Market system health

Thriving in uncertain markets

Figure 2.1: Leaders who want to thrive in complex situations must take steps to develop agility and market system health.

Key takeaways from this chapter are:

- **Appreciate the interconnected ways in which systems work.** Doing so is essential for market system health and agility.

- **Embrace complexity** through four mind shifts that adjust the lens through which markets and marketing are viewed. These mind shifts leverage new language, analogies, and stories drawn from other turbulent environments, along with greater awareness of our cognitive biases.

- **Adjust your operations to implement pragmatic actions that deliver results.** ComplexityWise marketing describes adjustments to intelligence systems, organizations, and work methods and approaches to transformation that help enterprises engage with marketing's VUCA reality.

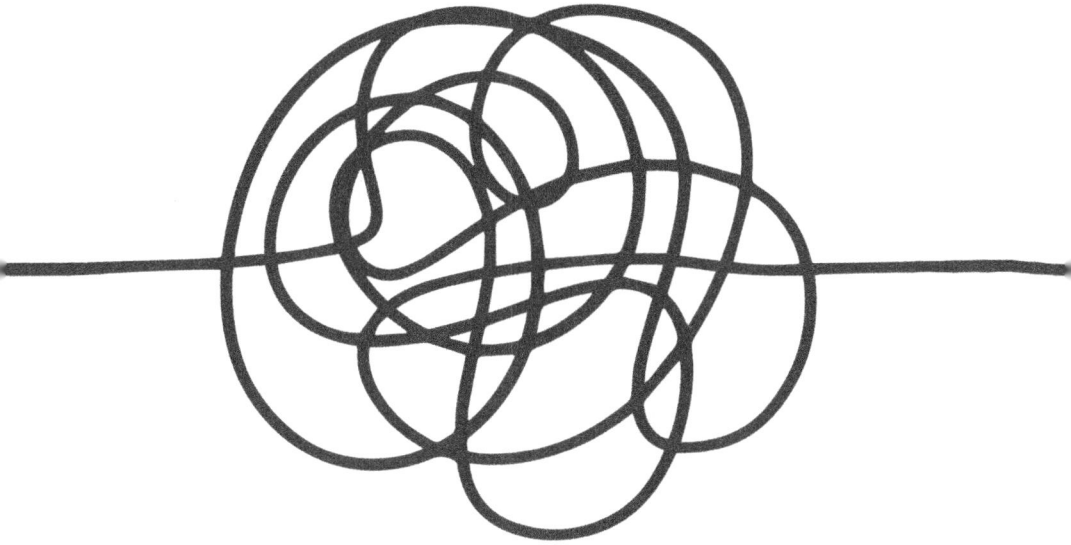

PART II

EMBRACING COMPLEXITY: FOUR MIND SHIFTS

The different actions required to thrive in the unpredictable world of marketing won't be possible until we start thinking differently. The following chapters delve into the four mind shifts that will enable the different actions described in part III. Here is a quick preview:

- **Think Like an Investor:** The first mind shift directs leaders away from an accounting perspective that marketing is a cost center where funds are spent and moves toward an investor's mindset where marketing funds are risked for future benefit. We can learn from the stock market, another complex system. Thinking like an investor is explored in chapter 3.

- **Think Like a Navigator:** The second mind shift demonstrates the shortcoming of a scorekeeping mentality that assumes future performance can be adequately measured against today's plans and moves toward embracing a navigator's acceptance of a constantly changing environment where plans and measurement must be flexible. The navigator mindset is inspired by the complex physical world of sailing, flying, and simply maneuvering through traffic. Thinking like a navigator is explored in chapter 4.

- **Think Like a Statistician:** The third mind shift recommends relinquishing the futile search for certainty and accepting that all future outcomes are probabilities. This mind shift requires more effort than the first two because human brains don't naturally think in probabilities. Quite the opposite, we love our cause-and-effect stories. Marketing outcomes do have causes, but they are not the clear reasons our brains crave. Thinking like a statistician helps managers realize that while no outcome is certain, markets do have patterns and as such are *semi*predictable, the way traffic and weather are semipredictable. Thinking like a statistician is explored in chapter 5.

- **Think Like an Ecologist:** The fourth mind shift guides leaders away from attempting to direct the success of individuals as isolated components of the organizational machine to a mindset focused on people as elements in an interconnected system. The leader's new goal is to create an optimal environment (ecosystem) for marketing success by fostering a beneficial environment where all the elements thrive together. In a VUCA world, those organizations that best foster the human capability to problem-solve, innovate, collaborate, and create will be most successful. Thinking like an ecologist is explored in chapter 6.

These four chapters challenge beliefs and practices you've likely honed during years spent in marketing. So my request to you is to approach these new mindsets with an open mind. Humans are sense-making creatures. We need a narrative of "the way the world works" to operate, and since we all learned our business acumen in the mostly industrial framework, the conventional ways of thinking and doing will feel most comfortable and make most sense to us. It may be difficult to imagine how things could be any other way.

Not everything devised in the industrial era goes away. Some perspectives can add value. A "yes, and" approach brought to fame in improv circles is more effective than an "either, or" mentality, and an inclusive method encourages sophisticated learning. Thriving in complexity requires us to be able to hold sometimes opposing ideas in our minds at the same time. Screen time for kids is educational *and* screen time for kids wrecks their creativity and attention span. Efficiency is good for business *and* efficiency causes problems for effectiveness in VUCA markets.

CHAPTER 3

THINK LIKE AN INVESTOR: FROM COST CENTER TO INVESTMENT

Forecasts are enticing to us because they provide crystal-clear answers to our most pressing problems. But they are mostly an exercise in taking recent history and extrapolating it into the future in a straight line. Life, as you know, is rarely made up of straight lines.

—David Gardener and Tom Gardener,
The Motley Fool Investment Guide

The first mind shift toward ComplexityWise marketing provides a fresh way to think about the marketing budget that will enhance agility and support market system health. This shift in executives' perspective is away from the traditional view of marketing as an efficiency-oriented cost center where the marketing budget is spent to acquire goods or services to one where today's funds are risked with the objective of gaining a larger-than-expected value over time. In this chapter, I talk about why the typical cost center mentality leads to problems in marketing's VUCA world and recommend four mindsets that will help you adopt an investor's way of thinking.

To be an investor is to think about the future. The mind shift to thinking like an investor takes its inspiration from stock market investors and venture capitalists, both of which operate in complex systems. Business leaders need to ask the same questions of marketing that stock investors ask—how can we amplify reward while reducing unnecessary risk, and how can we make investment decisions about our resources rationally and with as little bias as possible?

It's true that guidance from FASB (Financial Accounting Standards Board) directs managers to treat marketing expenditures as a cost, matching current spending with current gains. Reporting needs to remain consistent with legal requirements. But that's where the cost center mentality must end.

WHY A COST CENTER ORIENTATION NO LONGER WORKS

Cost is revenue-*taking*. To have a cost mentality is to think like a consumer, spending money on a product or service that gets used up and has fleeting value. Cost orientation is understandable. Waiting is tough for pragmatic businesspeople. Businesspeople hate to spend money, and reducing costs is a universal efficiency goal. If you view the marketing budget as a cost and, therefore, revenue-taking, it's natural to question expenditures that have no guaranteed results and hunger to recover it as soon as possible. But the cost orientation for marketing budgets possesses two fundamental flaws.

The first flaw relates to time lag. A cost orientation assumes that the items you spend money on have a predictable, fixed return and the timing of payoffs can be identified. Examples of costs and their returns include rent (where you get a month of space for your money), office supplies (a ream of paper), and utility bills (a month of electricity). However, marketing assets create value asynchronously. Payoff timing cannot be known in advance and only sometimes occurs within the current period.[1] Time lag is especially confounding for marketing assets aimed at improving company reputation and brand value and in B2B companies with long sales cycles.

Market success rarely progresses evenly. It can rush, then stall, and even go backward, then creep forward again. Lags and unevenness can cause executives to prematurely halt campaigns and fire CMOs—often right before they return their biggest results. This happens partly because most marketers can't get their hands on the historical data and analytics capability needed to discover correlations[2] between actions and outcomes spread over a protracted period, and like weather prediction, even with extensive data, the results will never be perfect.

The second flaw in the cost center orientation relates to risk. The cost mindset assumes a linear cost-benefit relationship where costs and benefits consistently relate. Volume discounts and quality differences notwithstanding, with expenditures, you get what you pay for. While there may be some risk in a purchase (will we really use up this box of paper before the end of the quarter?), the array of possible outcomes can be known, and managers can reasonably estimate their probability. The purpose of marketing funds, on the other hand, is to influence people, and this outcome is uncertain (a.k.a. risky) even in the best circumstances. Outcomes are subject to the effects of complex systems (e.g., non-linearity, emergence, interdependence). Costs and benefits don't consistently align, the range of outcomes cannot be completely known, and the probability of known outcomes is only estimated.

WHY AN INVESTMENT ORIENTATION WORKS BETTER

Investments are revenue-*making*. The investment mindset is generative. Like investments in the stock market, marketing delivers the biggest share of its value in the future. Very little of marketing's value is realized within the same period as it's purchased. While marketing has an important role as a short-term sales booster, its most essential role is developing long-term, compounding value. Due to non-linearity (the butterfly effect), early interventions produce disproportionately large future impact.

Here's a simple scenario: If you pay $500 for a piece of marketing content and it converts $500 in sales in the first month, you have already achieved a 1–1 return. But value creation from that content doesn't stop there. The asset remains in the market continuously selling. If by month six the content has returned $5000, your cost is still $500 and now your return is 1–10. While nothing lasts forever and the value of marketing assets eventually declines, some assets have remarkably long shelf lives. The longest-running TV ad, according to the Guinness World Records, has been running since 1975 by a tire company in Arizona.[3]

Marketing investments pay off in sales over time, and they can also reap more substantial rewards, including shareholder value. A 2018 study[4] published in the *British Journal of Management* looked at the investments and returns for US firms in various industries and sizes between the years 2004–2014. The study found that very low marketing investment does not increase shareholder value, and there is some indication that very low investment can detract. However, once investment reaches a level of sufficiency, it makes a positive impact on shareholder value, and after that point, more marketing investment continues to improve shareholder value.

Of course, every analogy has its limits and there are two ways that funding marketing differs from stock market investments.

- **Liquidity:** Stock market investors can buy and sell stocks mostly at will. Investment in marketing is more like venture capital in that, once committed, it works best if you are in for the distance. Marketing is a marathon, not a sprint, and continuous investment in a sound strategy has the best chance of producing results. Some periodic variation can be tolerated, but overall, CFOs who deploy an investment orientation lose the flexibility to use the marketing budget as a stash of liquid funds.

- **Separateness:** A single stock in a portfolio produces discrete value. Investors can buy or sell individual assets without impacting the others. Marketing programs, on the other hand, intertwine asset impact, and the value of one asset contributes to the value of others.

Due to these differences, managers need to take care not to push the comparison of stock investing to an extreme.

HOW TO THINK LIKE AN INVESTOR

There are four ways of thinking like an investor that are important when it comes to positioning marketing to thrive in a VUCA world:

1. Accept that payoffs are never guaranteed
2. Diversify investments
3. Play the long game
4. Balance efficiency with strategic slack

In this section, I walk through each of these mindsets and show how they contribute to effective marketing leadership.

Accept that Payoffs Are Never Guaranteed

Anytime you invest in a market, you take a risk. Investors aim to earn a higher payoff to compensate for this risk. Some marketing investments contain less risk than others. Which ones depends on the company and the context, and of course, it's wise to seek strategies that optimize reward and reduce risk.

But no investment has zero risk, and although every investor wants to say they are a long-term investor, market gyrations produce anxiety. "Long-term success has more to do with the ability to constantly shrug your shoulders at the world's unpredictability than it does constantly being right," advises the Motley Fool.[5] No one has ever figured out how to predict the ups and downs of markets. We would love to see the value of our 401(k)s rise each year, but since World War II, bear markets (declines of 20 percent or more) have occurred approximately every three to four years.[6] Product markets tend to be less volatile than highly liquid stock markets, but they can develop more slowly or quickly than anticipated. Being an investor requires patience. You don't want to abandon well-founded marketing strategies too soon.

Diversify Investments

Although all marketing investments involve some risk, it only makes sense to reduce that risk where possible. One risk-lowering strategy used by investors is diversification. Diversification won't reduce the risk of any individual thing going wrong, but it does mitigate systemic risk by reducing the likelihood that everything in the portfolio will go wrong at the same time or be equally subject to the same pressures. In complex systems, monolithic strategies are brittle and should be avoided.

In today's marketing arena with its expanding range of options for media and program types, rarely do marketing managers put "all their eggs in one basket." If anything, marketing is at risk for spreading investments too thinly and too randomly than being too concentrated. However, sometimes companies think they are diversifying by deploying the same strategy—frequently, short-term lead generation—in multiple channels while ignoring other strategies such as brand building or customer loyalty.

Because the different elements of a marketing portfolio influence the way others contribute to value, the proportion of various investments matters. Models can help with this decision. In the stock investing world, many institutions use something like the Modern Portfolio Theory[7] or the Yale Endowment Portfolio Model, both of which recommend investing in a diverse set of asset classes with varying risk-reward profiles to assist with the smooth funding of their operating model. As an illustration, the Yale model, in June 2020, contained a balance of 22.6 percent venture capital, 21.6 percent absolute return, 15.8 percent leverage buyouts, 13.7 percent cash and fixed income, 11.4 percent foreign equity, 8.6 percent real estate, 3.9 percent natural resources, and 2.3 percent domestic equity. Each year, Yale adjusts the percentages to respond to market trends and conditions.[8]

When I ran IDC's annual marketing investment survey, we found that the best performing[9] technology companies kept important ratios in balance. Some ratios stayed stable over many years. For example, the average sales-to-marketing cost envelope for B2B tech companies (including people, programs, and specifically named support elements) remained roughly 80 percent cost of sales to 20 percent cost of marketing. However, other ratios evolved. One ratio that consistently increased was the percent of revenue spent on marketing. Also, the proportion of the marketing programs budget spent on digital marketing moved from 19 percent in 2010 to 48 percent in 2019.[10]

Ratios differed somewhat depending on company size, industry sector, and business model. (See sidebar B2B Brand Advertising.) When a company's marketing stumbled, the problem diagnosis was often found in budget allocations that were too off-kilter for their business model. One example is companies that cut people costs after a big layoff, leaving too few marketers to adequately manage the programs budget. Wise companies will find a marketing mix that works well for them and manage the balance while monitoring and changing the mix to adapt to current needs.

A lot of investing wisdom comes down to avoiding catastrophic mistakes rather than picking winners every time. Peter Lynch, investor, mutual fund manager, and author of the wildly successful book *One Up on Wall Street* says, "You don't need to make money on every stock you pick. In my experience, six out of ten winners in a portfolio can produce a satisfying result . . . All you need for a lifetime of successful investing is a few big winners, and the pluses from those will overwhelm the minuses from stocks that don't work out."[11]

Venture capital portfolios experience a range of success rates. Scott Kupor, author and managing partner at Andreessen Horowitz, discusses how only a small percent of companies they invest in capture the lion's share of return, while the rest are mediocre or duds. As an illustration, Kupor reports that VCs lose at least some money in a full 50 percent of their investments, and 20–30 percent of investments are the equivalent of baseball singles or doubles (e.g., earning 2x–4x investment). These returns aren't bad, but they are not enough to compensate for losses in the lowest 50 percent. Only 10–20 percent of VC investments are home runs, and these are the ones that matter.[12]

Even if marketers could make great decisions every time and execute exceptionally, outcomes will still vary. Diversification helps mitigate the risk of these normal patterns.

SIDEBAR: B2B BRAND ADVERTISING

The rigorous data-driven work of advertising authorities Les Binet and Peter Field has drawn links between efforts to improve share of voice and share of market. For more than two decades, the UK IPA[13] (Institute of Practitioners in Advertising) has studied and published best practices related to advertising.

In recent years, the practice of brand advertising as a growth driver has lost traction, even in B2C companies where advertising long reigned, in favor of what Binet and Field say are the "exaggerated claims" of performance marketing. Managers in B2B are especially skeptical, believing that although gullible consumers may be swayed by advertising, B2B decision-making is rational.

In a 2021 study for the B2B Institute,[14] Field and Binet say that most companies can forego brand-building in their early days when sales of innovative products tend to grow through word-of-mouth along with an industrious sales force and good customer service. But eventually, growth hits an inflection point and diminishes. The math behind this S-shaped curve describes the effect of a dwindling number of new adopters as a market matures. Once they hit this inflection point, companies need advertising to spur further growth. This pattern has been demonstrated in B2C companies, and the institute's 2021 report, "The Five Principles of Growth in B2B Marketing," demonstrates the same pattern in B2B.

Brand advertising reduces price sensitivity and creates emotional experiences that last longer than demand tactics. Demand marketing converts, but the effects die out almost immediately. The IPA Databank found that the optimal ratio of budget allocated to brand vs. sales activation varied by business model. Rule of thumb: B2C companies can use a 60:40 split and B2B 50:50.

Play the Long Game

Time is on the investor's side. "Play the long game" is the guidance trusted investment advisors give clients because investments compound over time, and due to non-linearity, early investments have a larger-than-expected impact on future results. Entrepreneurs are often surprised that venture capitalists are generally involved with their portfolio companies for five to ten years or longer. To paraphrase a business adage: Sales (the short game) is asking someone to marry you; marketing (the long game) is what makes them say yes.

A common response to the challenge of waiting is to ignore the time lag and slide into short-termism. The Oxford dictionary defines short-termism as the "concentration on short-term projects or objectives for immediate profit at the expense of long-term security."[15] Part of short-termism derives from our biology. Human brains become addicted to the dopamine released with immediate gratification, and it takes training, experience, and a cool head to appreciate the value of building long-term wealth. Practices such as the urgency of quarterly earnings exacerbates the tendency to choose short-term rewards.

In certain situations, there can be practical reasons for short-termism. One reason is when companies expect an imminent revenue shortfall. Or a company may suspect they won't be in business long enough to reap the benefits of long-term investment because they hope to be acquired soon. Used infrequently and under appropriate conditions, a short-term concentration may be effective, but there is a price to pay. The longer short-termism lasts, the less sales will be bolstered by earlier investments.

Paving the road to a sale starts well before it's culmination. Many things must be true for a sale to happen. Prospective buyers must be motivated. They need questions answered. They must trust the vendor. They need social validation that the decision they are about to make is a good one. If a sales cycle is six months, how long before that does a company need to start cultivating references? If a buyer has thirty questions, how long does it take to learn what those questions are, prepare persuasive answers, and figure out how to get them to interested buyers? How long will it take to build a website that inspires curiosity and confidence or to develop an online presence that sparks when buyers search for answers? How long does it take to understand customers and tailor experiences that serve? How long does it take to nurture a reputation so solid that when a wobbly buyer balked, someone trusted stepped in to assure, "Don't worry; they're good people"? When you stop investing in marketing foundations, sales momentum leaks away.

Balance Efficiency with Strategic Slack

Underlying the traditional cost-oriented mindset is the drive for efficiency. Every businessperson acknowledges the pitfalls of inefficiency: wasted money, squandered time, lower profits. Given the importance that efficiency has attained in earnings discussions, it's no wonder executives and stock pickers are hyper-focused on a company's performance on this metric.

When operating in complex systems, like markets, managers must also be alert to the hazards of excessive efficiency. Therefore, this is a case where investing in marketing is more like a venture capitalist who understands that too much efficiency at the wrong time cuts future growth off at the knees. The idiom "too much of a good thing" reaches back hundreds of years, implying that even generally beneficial things turn toxic if overapplied. In marketing, both ends of the resource spectrum—too much slack and too much efficiency—are risky positions. Too much efficiency reduces both agility and resilience.

Slack, or float, is the term used by project managers to describe the amount of time flexibility or delay that can be tolerated before the project completion is impacted. Strategic slack is the conscious infusion of extra resources—time, money, or other assets—to progress an important objective regardless of whether that investment has short-term payback.

Productivity is an important goal, and marketers are expected to deliver campaigns quickly to demonstrate productivity. It's true that speediness is more efficient than delay, but a little intentional float in the schedule provides the flexibility to recover from delays, absorb change, regenerate, repair, and learn. Time-slack also gives teams an opportunity to experiment and generate innovative new ideas.

CFOs are sometimes proud of how little they spend on marketing, but budget-slack, that is, adding a little more money than ROI analysis would suggest, matters more than you can prove. When analyzing IDC's annual marketing investment survey, we found that running marketing too tightly, with too little budget compared to peers, correlated with lower revenue growth. My observation after many discussions with marketing leaders on the topic is this: Starving marketers can only keep the lights on. At the request of their CEO, one CMO asked me to analyze their spending data for insight on why their marketing wasn't working. I found his budget to be among the lowest I had seen, which forced the CMO to make hard choices on what to forego.

Consider how poverty impacts families. Even just a little extra money provides better healthcare, more education, less stress on relationships, and the ability to weather downturns. My poverty-stricken CMO client was unable to adequately invest in the technology necessary to compete and couldn't experiment with new campaigns to find more effective messaging or offer sufficient education to their retail partners. The CEO defended his decision to spend very little on marketing, blaming the company's lack of profitability, an understandable rationalization. However, the decision sent the company into a downward spiral.

In addition to time and money, slack in other areas can also be beneficial for agility and market system health. Taylor's scientific management preached uniformity as more efficient than diversity, but innovation benefits from a wider range of ideas and backgrounds. Failsafe is more efficient than experimentation, but safe-to-fail is needed for discovering adaptations to constant change. An example comparing two campaigns demonstrates how a bit more strategic slack can offer benefits.

Emma and Ahmad both conduct campaigns with a $10,000 budget. Emma's campaign produces better ROI in the short-term than Ahmad's because her campaign produces one hundred leads, leading to $100,000 in revenue in three months, while his produces only eighty leads, leading to $80,000 in revenue in the same period. Here are some possible elements that don't show up on a typical ROI analysis that, if present, show why Ahmad's campaign is a better choice.

- **New business development:** Ahmad's campaign may produce leads from several "net new logo" accounts that later turn out to be lucrative, while Emma's simply exposes existing deals from current customers.

- **Innovation:** Ahmad could experiment with a new artificial intelligence capability in the company's martech (marketing technology) stack, leading to useful departmental insights, while Emma repeats known tactics.

- **Improved customer experience:** Ahmad's campaign may delight customers leading to better Net Promoter Scores (NPS) and larger deals over time. Emma's, unfortunately, produces "collateral damage" by spamming some of her prospects.

- **Resilience:** Ahmad's campaign may involve retail partners, thus improving their business and increasing their capabilities, while Emma's makes none of these improvements.

Every company should try to find a balance. Strive for enough efficiency to avoid chaos and achieve reasonable competitiveness while allowing enough strategic slack to improve agility, innovation, customer experience, and resilience. Figure 3.1 illustrates the risks of moving too far in either direction.

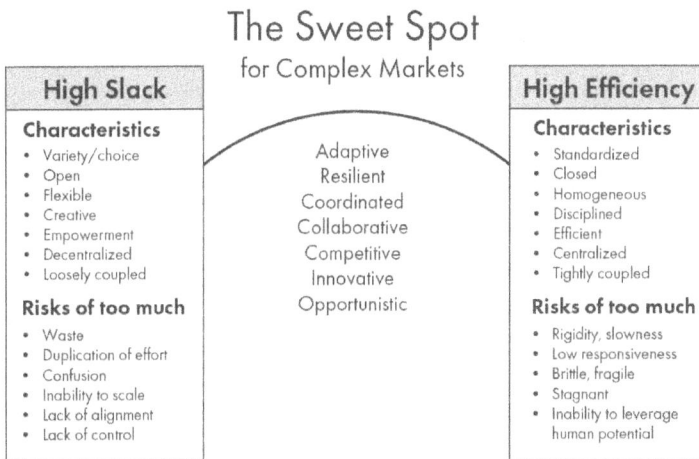

The Sweet Spot
for Complex Markets

High Slack		High Efficiency
Characteristics	Adaptive	**Characteristics**
• Variety/choice	Resilient	• Standardized
• Open	Coordinated	• Closed
• Flexible	Collaborative	• Homogeneous
• Creative	Competitive	• Disciplined
• Empowerment	Innovative	• Efficient
• Decentralized	Opportunistic	• Centralized
• Loosely coupled		• Tightly coupled
Risks of too much		**Risks of too much**
• Waste		• Rigidity, slowness
• Duplication of effort		• Low responsiveness
• Confusion		• Brittle, fragile
• Inability to scale		• Stagnant
• Lack of alignment		• Inability to leverage
• Lack of control		human potential

Figure 3.1: Finding a Balance Between Slack and Efficiency

COGNITIVE BIASES THAT INTERFERE WITH INVESTOR THINKING

If you desire to think like an investor, it will be helpful to be aware of two universal cognitive biases—loss aversion and ownership bias—which can lead investors to miscalculate risk. Cognitive biases swing our thinking in predictable directions, like the aforementioned arrow that always lands in the same off-center location. While sometimes that misdirection works in our favor, it's wise to be aware of bias so that you can course correct when you choose.

Loss Aversion ("What if it doesn't work?")—We all hate losing money; that's natural. Loss aversion is the cognitive imbalance that distorts that distaste, causing us to feel the pain of losing $10,000 more than we feel happy about the gain of $10,000. The aversion to potential regret can lead investors to take less risk than is reasonably warranted. Marketing leaders experiencing loss aversion may avoid the risk of trying new things for fear of poor outcomes. CFOs may demand a higher degree of predictive proof from marketing than is practical, realistic, or even wise.

To guard against this bias, accept that when you invest in marketing you *might* lose your investment, no question. But as the saying goes, "You must be present to win." Taking ComplexityWise action—one that is skillful, not impulsive, and is adaptive to the current situation—gives you an opportunity to benefit from the upside should your gamble pay off.

Ownership Bias ("But we'll lose all that money!")—The greater the investment we've made, the more we tend to cling to it. Ownership bias leads us to overvalue ideas, practices, and items we've previously spent resources on. Related to ownership bias is the sunk-cost bias, which describes why we often fail to walk away from investments that aren't working out. Accepting defeat and the waste of resources is difficult.

As we put more time, money, sweat, or tears into something, it becomes more special to us, but others don't see it that way. Once, I shopped at a peddler's faire for a vintage trunk my daughter wanted. When I found one trunk that I thought she would love, the seller quoted me a price nearly four times what I had found elsewhere. I was willing to pay a premium for the trunk's good condition and to avoid further search, but the price was outrageous. When I protested, the seller revealed his ownership bias. He highly valued the trunk because he had put so much work into fixing it up and he wanted his work to be compensated. As a customer, I looked at the trunk's value comparison with alternatives—his time didn't matter to me. I walked on and later found a nice choice at a fair market price.

Due to ownership bias and sunk-cost bias, businesspeople may hang on to products, campaigns, or media choices long after letting go makes sense. To fight this bias, embrace the concept that letting go will free up resources for better opportunities.

TAKE THIS AWAY

Marketing budgets are powerful levers for directing the course of a marketing organization. To thrive in a VUCA reality, it's essential that leaders move away from the traditional view of marketing as an efficiency-oriented cost center, where the marketing budget is spent to acquire goods or services in the here and now, to one where current funds are risked with the objective of gaining a larger-than-expected value over time. With this shift, companies win the opportunity to harvest marketing's greatest benefits. With an investment mindset, marketing will become more agile and the company's market system health will increase.

Key takeaways from this chapter are:

- **Payoffs aren't guaranteed.** Anytime you invest in a market, you take a risk. Investors aim to earn a higher payoff to compensate for this risk. Seek strategies that optimize reward when opportunity presents itself and reduce risk where possible.

- **Diversify.** Diversification doesn't reduce the risk of any individual thing going wrong, but it does mitigate systemic risk by reducing the likelihood that everything in the portfolio will go wrong at the same time or be equally subject to the same pressures.

- **"Play the long game"** is the guidance trusted investment advisors give clients because investments compound over time, and due to non-linearity, early investments can have a larger-than-expected impact on future results.

- **Aim for an efficiency sweet spot** that allows for some strategic slack, the conscious infusion of extra resources to progress an important objective regardless of whether that investment has short-term payback.

- Become aware of when the cognitive biases (of **loss aversion** and the **ownership bias**) may be playing an inappropriate role in marketing resource decisions.

CHAPTER 4

THINK LIKE A NAVIGATOR: FROM SCOREKEEPER TO ORIENTEER

*The wind and the waves are always on
the side of the ablest navigators.*

—**Attributed to Edmund Gibbon,** *English historian*

The second ComplexityWise mind shift directs perspective away from the traditional view of markets as stable places where marketing's success can be scored against detailed advance plans and toward a navigator's realm where the marketing plan and the interpretation of scores must be continually adapted due to perpetual change.

Navigation is about finding our way. We all feel anxious about which step to take when the future is unclear. Professional odysseys often fall into this category. I have mentored dozens of marketers as they navigated their career paths, and even after years of experience, they wonder about their best next step and how they will gauge if they are making the right moves.

Every year, marketers face a similar directional predicament when developing the annual plan. They face questions such as: Should we extend last year's strategy or try something innovative? What go-to-market campaign will best entice customers toward a purchase? What approach will jumpstart a product line where sales have stalled?

The navigator's mindset takes inspiration from those who maneuver through the physical world's fluctuations. To think like a navigator is to approach the market as though it were a continually shifting ocean or buffeting air currents. There are no straight lines from here to there in the physical world. Whether sailing the ocean, flying through clouds, or simply winding through traffic, the navigator's mindset *assumes* that what is ahead will surprise and thus prioritizes vigilant observation, constant learning, and the ability to course correct as quickly as the environment shifts.

All good marketing leaders do plenty of planning and lots of measurement! "Plans are useless, but planning is indispensable," said former American President and Army General Dwight Eisenhower.[1] Regardless of whether a plan is ever executed, planning calms anxiety about the uncertain future enough to allow thoughtful, coordinated movement. What must be challenged is the traditional relationship of advance planning to the way plans are worked and measured. How that changes when variability and unpredictability come into the mix is the subject of this chapter.

WHY SCOREKEEPING DOESN'T WORK FOR MARKETING

The traditional approach to planning works like this: Build the plan, work the plan, and measure progress against the plan. Plans typically start at an organizational pinnacle where senior executives hammer down the strategy and high-level objectives, then send the plan cascading down the hierarchy. The next level functional leaders identify required initiatives, painfully try to interlock with peers, and wrestle with what resources will be needed. Once these tasks are complete, specific actions and performance objectives trickle down to workers. Once it's done, the plan is routinely monitored. Key Performance Indicators (KPIs) measure how well the plan is executed and whether it meets predicted results.

This process works decently in slow-moving, reliable environments, but the traditional method has three flaws when applied in dynamic markets.

The first flaw is that every advance marketing plan is wrong. Volatility guarantees that the market will have already changed even before the plan is complete. This is especially true in companies that take months to complete their process. Some markets evolve more slowly than others, but none are exempt. Plans are also always wrong because planners, being human, can't help but distort the plan with their cognitive biases, such as the "well-traveled road effect," which describes the tendency to underestimate the time and resources it takes to do familiar things and overestimate the effort to do the unfamiliar.

Second, traditional planning is more wasteful than planners realize because this method heavily relies on getting things right in advance (after all, people's performance is being scored against it). Planners exert tremendous time, effort, and resources to try to perfect something that will always be wrong. Then, while the marketing team focuses on executing the original plan, they may not see the unexpected but lucrative opportunities that pass by. And if the plan misses a market shift, there is the price of recovery, which was inevitably not in the budget.

Third, conflict occurs when marketing plans, which were supposed to be accurate, miss their mark. Fingers get pointed, scapegoats are fired, and employees become resentful. Managers who love control are especially prone to disappointment. Some disappointments are minor, such as when a campaign gets fewer responses than the demand team had hoped. Others are devastating, such as when the "bet the company" product fails or the expensive new website gets hate mail from customers.

WHY A NAVIGATOR'S ORIENTATION WORKS BETTER

A navigator's mindset is responsive to their evolving context. Navigators view the process of planning as essential, but since the physical world constantly changes, they expect to continually adapt plans and have built into their routine methods to do so. While every journey has a resolute purpose, such as a mission or a desired destination, the navigator understands that the how and when of the journey must be at least somewhat flexible.

It's the navigator's job to move everyone safely through this shifting terrain to achieve their purpose. The navigator guides the development of the trip plan and then, while on-route, maintains awareness of the craft's location and finds whatever can be known about what is up ahead. The navigator advises the pilot on things such as the timing to destination and how to avoid potential hazards. Today's navigators use a multitude of tools to inform the maneuvering and monitor the impact of the turbulent environmental factors such as tides, currents, and weather.

Marketing navigators work in a similar way. Trends and patterns in the feedback data contribute insights for optimal next steps. Just as ships and planes need to change course if the situation requires, so to do marketing plans require continual adjustments with different plan elements evolving at appropriate rates. KPIs become such navigation tools, providing directional indicators about whether the team is getting closer or further away from the mission, which includes, among other things, the company's financial goals.

HOW TO THINK LIKE A NAVIGATOR

There are four patterns of thinking common to navigators that are critical for marketing in today's world:

1. Iterate your plans by wayfinding

2. Think in varying time scales

3. Seek frequent feedback

4. Don't get attached to precise outcomes

In this section, I explain how each of these approaches work and how they contribute to marketing success.

Iterate Your Plans by Wayfinding

Planning in a predictable environment is very straightforward: You can create plans using a linear process, then implement them after everything is finalized. (See top of figure 4.1.)

This linearity doesn't work for marketing. While previous experience and past data should inform your plan, these cannot prescribe your plan, because, as the saying goes, the past is not prologue. Instead, you must discover the forward path. Industrial designers use the term *wayfinding* to describe the discovery-oriented sequence of steps that humans use to navigate unfamiliar settings, such as trying to find a room in a strange hospital or a particular seat in a darkened theater. They take a small step, study the process and outcomes to learn what did and didn't work, adjust their direction accordingly, take another small step, and so on. (See bottom of figure 4.1.)

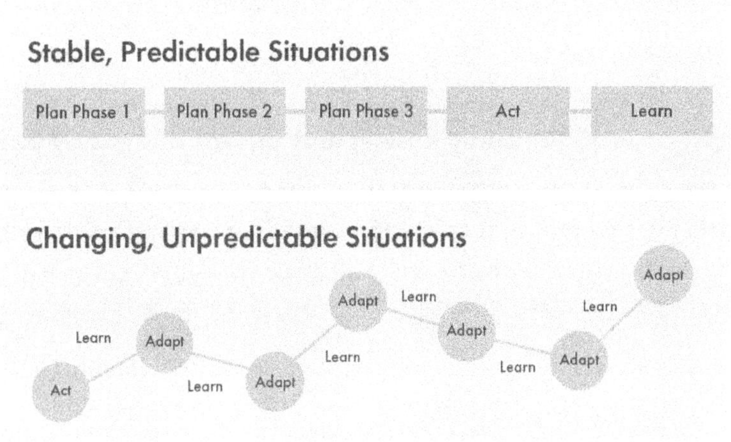

Stable, Predictable Situations

| Plan Phase 1 | Plan Phase 2 | Plan Phase 3 | Act | Learn |

Changing, Unpredictable Situations

Act — Learn — Adapt — Learn — Adapt — Learn — Adapt — Learn — Adapt — Learn — Adapt — Learn — Adapt

Figure 4.1: How Planning Differs in Stable vs. Variable Environments

Wayfinding improves the accuracy of motion and reduces the risk of error. The process can be summarized in three steps:

Step 1—Act: Take a best-guess first step. The path of discovery in wayfinding starts with the Nike-coined advice, "Just do it." Marketers should adopt a bias toward action. Many people freeze when faced with uncertainty or think they should wait to get fully informed. But in a changing environment, you don't get smarter by waiting. As a marketer I know humorously commented on a LinkedIn post, "It's like someone is about to be run over by a giant boulder, and everyone is screaming 'Run!' and the person is saying, 'Wait, I'm trying to fully grasp the situation.'"

Early Polynesian explorers used a type of wayfinding when they island-hopped in the vast Pacific Ocean using no technical guidance tools. These navigators could never establish an idealized route to the tiny speck of Tahiti because they could not anticipate how the wind, currents, and weather would impact their canoes. Instead of following a set plan that attempted a single long-haul beeline to an ambiguous far-away destination, they would set off in the general direction—east, for example—aiming for easier-to-find waypoints, archipelagos that could be used to orient them toward the desired island. Interim steps that reveal additional insight are ideal. For example, a CMO might choose to conduct a small pilot to learn about a new market.

Step 2—Learn: Vigilantly observe and analyze your experience. Any action taken in an uncertain environment is a hypothesis, a starting place for further investigation. Therefore, wayfinding emphasizes information gathering and analysis to aid inevitable course correction. As the Polynesian explorers navigated, along the way they gathered situational knowledge from the sun and stars and from the behavior of porpoises, seagulls, and wave patterns to inform their next step.

In the early days of the COVID pandemic, when there was high uncertainty about when in-person events would resume, one company found that hinging their planning cadence on milestones versus calendars was a good strategy for taking small, insightful steps. The global events team met daily to identify when the next big decision point would occur for the events in its portfolio. Rather than attempt to create a hard-and-fast policy for when to schedule expensive events, they redirected choices one milestone at a time. Their first decision came early in the spring of 2020, when they faced whether to put a large down payment on a hotel block for an October partner event in Germany. They decided to pause that event, monitor the situation, and periodically revisit their decision.

Step 3—Adapt: Modify your plan based on what you've learned. Eventually, the tech company cut the big event format in favor of smaller regional and hybrid formats that could be tailored to the unique situations in various countries. Polynesian navigators would adjust their direction as needed at each interim waypoint based on the information gathered along the way until they reached their destination.

Marketers will find that many of their modifications will be small because market changes tend to be maddeningly faint yet constant, like rivers as they carve canyons. A CMO once told me that good marketing work can be boring for marketers because it should depend on a consistent stream of small changes rather than exciting but risky big bangs. Only occasionally does life thrust a boulder onto one's path that requires radical transformation. The challenge is to notice subtle changes. It's easy, especially for very experienced people, to gloss over small changes and assume things in the environment are the same. But things are always changing. It's only in hindsight we see how different things have become, and by then, recovery is expensive.

EXAMPLES OF WAYFINDING

Agile software developers use a version of wayfinding. Their initial step is to get just good-enough usable code, known as *minimum viable*, into users' hands as quickly as possible. Then they iterate to adjust and improve. The Scientific Method[2] is also a form of wayfinding. Scientists ask questions, gather information, form hypotheses, test with experiments, analyze and draw conclusions, compare results with the hypothesis, communicate and discuss results. This process is repeated, and scientists assume that what they know is theoretical ("true for now"), accepting that there is always more to be learned.

Think in Varying Time Scales

Everything changes in a complex market, but not everything changes at the same pace. However, typical market planning treats everything the same, iterating annually, with everything marching to the dominant tempo of the financial calendar. But this cadence isn't appropriate for all aspects of marketing.

In the book *The Clock of the Long Now: Time and Responsibility*,[3] author Stewart Brand, an American writer, editor, and entrepreneur, explains how nature's ecosystems absorb the shock of change because of varying speeds of adaptation. Some elements change quickly ("fast learns") while others change slowly ("slow remembers"). The balance of these varying time scales produces resilience. Pine needles on individual trees in a conifer forest change yearly, while the tree crown unfolds over several years, and the overall forest ecosystem evolves over thousands of years. This multilayered evolution allows the system to absorb stresses like parasites and weather.[4]

Brand describes a six-layered model of civilizational order (figure 4.2), where each layer plays a critical role in society's health. The top layer, which he calls *fashion*, works like this: "The job of fashion and art is to be froth: quick, irrelevant, engaging, self-preoccupied, and cruel. Try this! No, no, try *this!*"[5] Fashion and art, Brand says, should be free to experiment as creatively and irresponsibly as society can bear. Commerce—the business activity layer—sits below fashion, and it is fashion's froth that drives commerce's energy. The next four layers—infrastructure, governance, culture, and finally nature—evolve more slowly. Businesses can find the measured pace of the lower levels frustrating. For example, most marketers will be familiar with complaints about how the slow pace of the "people piece" (i.e., culture) impedes changes that executives want immediately. Yet, the slower changing forces are necessary to stabilize, and Brand says commercial entities must invest in the health of these sustaining layers to achieve optimal results. Allowing any layer to dominate, including commerce, is a recipe for calamity.

Pace Layering

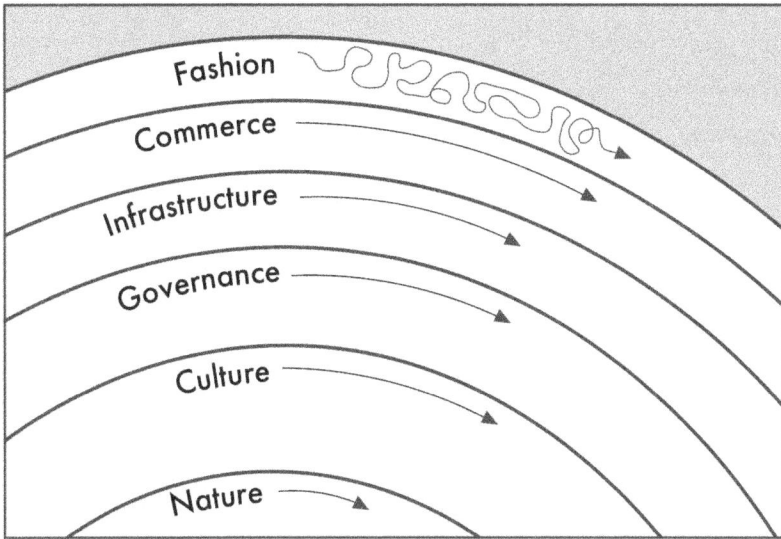

Figure 4.2: Variability in the Pace of Change

Source: Brand, S., 1999, *The Clock of the Long Now*, p.37

Market planning can be layered in this time-aware way. One company devised a process like the chart in table 4.A to ensure that plan elements were appropriately paced in multiple time intervals. Deconstructing planning from an annual behemoth yoked to the financial activities into layers pertinent to their rate of change allows plan elements to travel at optimal pacing.

This company's financial plan, which is analogous to Brand's commerce layer, must be completed annually or semiannually in accordance with legal requirements. However, they encouraged the more market-innovative and customer-responsive elements, represented by the Go-to-Market (GTM) and Program layers, to be (like fashion) freer to experiment, fail, and change more frequently in accordance with the tumult at the company's edge. Campaigns and sales plays should change faster than the company's financial calendar because faster iterations of wayfinding's act/learn/adapt sequence mean fewer changes occur between action and outcome, learning is quicker, less effort is wasted, and outcomes become more certain.

However, speeding up everything is a poor goal too. Other elements, the "remembering" aspects of the plan, such as the mission, strategy, brand, infrastructure, and organization, which are represented in the company's Strategic Layer, should change less frequently but, nonetheless, evolve.

Plan Layer	Description	Frequency	Examples
Strategic Layer	Strategic initiatives that move the company in significant new directions and take multiple years to come to fruition	*Development:* Every 5 years or as needed by disruptive events *Monitoring:* Workstreams parsed into annual/six month/ quarterly project modules and placed into the appropriate budget cycle	Brand strategy Building the Next Generation MarTech stack Preparing to serve new generations of "buyers and hires"
Commercial Layer	Financial plan for the company	*Development:* Every year *Monitoring:* Updated quarterly	Sales and profit by region, product line, etc. Budgets
Go-to-Market (GTM) Layer	Marketing plan to achieve the strategic and financial objectives. Initial plan is built concurrent with annual financial plan. Adjusted plan is built midway to optimize for 2nd half performance	*Development:* Every six months for major changes *Monitoring:* Quarterly reviews for minor changes. *Adaptation:* No program has a guaranteed budget as changing needs at the strategy, commercial, or program layers are reflected in the GTM budget	Campaigns Sales playbooks Events Milestone projects for long-term initiatives
Program Layer	Tactics and programs executed to deliver on the GTM plan	*Developed:* Continuously *Monitoring:* Continuously. Changed as often as needed and if possible, in near real-time	Sales plays Creative execution Digital programs

Table 4.A: Example of Pacing for Planning Components in an Unpredictable World

Seek Frequent Feedback

When maneuvering in uncertain environments, people make better decisions about where to go next if they can accurately see what is happening and what is up ahead. One of the most important tools of modern navigation is the Global Positioning System (GPS). Feedback in marketing gained from a wide range of sources serves as a type of GPS.

According to NASA.gov,[6] GPS receivers on a device constantly scan for signals from thirty-plus satellites that gather location data including latitude, longitude, and altitude. Once the receiver homes in on a signal from four or more satellites, it provides pilots or drivers with situational information. This continuous dialog between the GPS device and the satellites enables navigators to see the real-time implications of their local movements. When a driver turns, the system gives them immediate feedback about whether they are closer or farther away from the desired destination. Sometimes it provides information about conditions ahead.

The more uncertain the terrain and the faster conditions change, the more pilots, drivers, and marketers need feedback. In slow-moving, stable markets, marketers can probably manage with the knowledge they've gained from experience, just like a driver doesn't really need a GPS to get to a familiar supermarket. However, when marketers work in dynamic customer situations, they gain advantage from continuous and high-quality intelligence. The quicker and more accurately they can adjust to shifts, the less they will wobble from the optimal route, and more efficient will be their actions.

The strategic layers of marketing plans also benefit from feedback such as surveys, research, predictive analytics, and customer reviews. Hypothetical feedback can be gained from models such as Monte Carlo simulations, which are computer-based models that predict the probability of a range of outcomes when random variables are present, or scenario planning, which can be used to explore wildly divergent futures. Every hypothetical model or scenario will be at least somewhat wrong. However, they help companies visualize how they connect to the larger market and identify trigger points that signal impending change. A head start in a profitable direction can have enormous value. An article in *Harvard Business Review*[7] discusses how an automotive manufacturer used scenario planning to determine that the penetration of battery-powered electric vehicles made a useful trigger point for decisions on how much to invest in traditional engines, size of their dealer network, etc. Based on this insight, they decided that their best move would be to shrink investment in traditional cars once EVs got to 30 percent penetration.

SIDEBAR: FEEDBACK IN A COMPLEX SYSTEM CREATES CRAZY OUTCOMES

Feedback in a business context typically means using data and getting opinions or advice from others. In complexity science, feedback has broader, further-reaching implications.

Every single interaction within a complex system influences other interactions, thus producing feedback. In a market system, these interactions can be physical or information exchanges. Time is no barrier. Interactions from the past influence the present and the future. The internet has been a game changer because it has accelerated feedback and vastly increased the number of connections and, thus, interactions and unintended consequences.

This feedback can create a reinforcing (positive) feedback loop, which amplifies the direction of the original action and creates a "snowball effect," or a balancing (negative) feedback loop, which redirects the energy of the interaction. An example of a positive feedback loop would be a viral media craze where the increasing popularity of an item drives even more people to buy it. An example of a negative feedback loop would be when a buyer changes their mind about a product based on reading an unfavorable review.

Imagine billions of these feedback loops happening around us and all the emanating consequences producing seemingly random outcomes. No wonder the complex system of marketing can be crazy!

Don't Get Attached to Precise Outcomes

Navigators almost always set out with a destination in mind. But what is a meaningful destination for marketing? CEOs think they know—the correct destination is whatever outcome is mandated in the plan. Nine out of ten CEOs say that the role of marketing is clearly defined, according to a 2023 McKinsey study.[8] However, only 22 percent of marketing chiefs agree. Executives set themselves up for disappointment when they set marketing objectives too precisely.

Executives should certainly set goals, but given marketing's VUCA reality, they might look to baseball for an example of how to flexibly think about and manage those goals. Every baseball player would love to have a batting average over .300, yet the fact that most of them don't achieve this excellence doesn't stop them from trying. Players aim to improve their average over time, all the while acknowledging that they will perform better in some seasons than others. Similarly, ComplexityWise marketers aim to improve the percentage, duration, and size of wins rather than worrying about exact scores. In addition to setting aspirational goals, leaders may decide to define a floor for the lowest acceptable rate of return.

VUCA markets can occasionally produce a streak of great metrics for average campaigns or poor results for great marketing. One example comes from a technology reseller that launched a campaign to attract senior IT professionals in a new market using local events. Attendance at the first event was much higher than average. Salespeople were able to meet with more prospects, leading to strong pipeline growth. Based on initial results, regional sales management wanted to immediately divert a large chunk of the field marketing budget to this new segment. Marketing was skeptical because although event attendance was high, statistical analysis showed that it was still within a normal probability range. The company continued to market to the new segment, but the initial great results were never repeated. Within a few months, outcomes within the new segment had sunk back to slightly lower-than-average pipeline return. This demonstrates how a single data point, or just a few, can be misleading. Tracking over time provides stronger evidence for a pivot or trend. Diverting more budget to this segment, as sales management had suggested, would have been a mistake.

Even lower-than-average metric performance may be acceptable under certain strategic conditions. Just as a start-up loses money in its first seasons, a new marketing venture may not have a positive ROI during the testing phase. In other cases, ROI may be a completely inappropriate metric because the marketing program is intended for a purpose other than revenue such as meeting regulatory, competitive, or customer experience requirements.

COGNITIVE BIASES THAT INTERFERE WITH NAVIGATION THINKING

If you desire to think like a navigator, it will be helpful to be aware of two universal cognitive biases—the normalcy bias and the frequency bias—that can lull navigators into false beliefs about the reality of change.

Normalcy Bias ("We've got this")—Just because something hasn't happened before doesn't mean it will never happen. Normalcy bias soothes us into thinking that the future will mimic the past. Most predictions, even by the most expert people, gravitate toward linear extensions of the current state. But the status quo rarely exists for long in a complex system.

While sudden shocks occasionally occur, such as the COVID pandemic or the 2008 Great Recession, the normalcy bias most often leaves us ignorant of the more commonplace *creeping change*—the gradual accumulation of small changes. Famously, Thomas Watson, chairman and CEO of IBM, missed the boat when he predicted in 1943 that the world might need maybe five computers because he failed to recognize changes in the world that would make more people want and need computers.

The riskiest aspect of the normalcy bias occurs when creeping change eats away at deeply held, cherished values and practices. I knew a handful of B2B executives who even just a few years ago still clung to their belief that buyers of big-ticket items will rarely purchase online, leading to dramatic underinvestment in digital marketing. Normalcy bias tricks managers into underpreparing for adaptation and resiliency.

To fight against this bias, teach yourself to look for clues that the future (next week, next month, next year) will be different from the status quo as you know it. Challenge yourself to question whether your plans or strategies are based on conditions staying the same—and, if so, what you can do to make them more adaptable given that change *will* happen.

Frequency Bias ("Things always happen in threes")—Once we notice change, we tend to look for patterns that indicate predictability in that change. While it is true that patterns exist in complex systems, these patterns aren't quite as simple and certain as our brain's frequency bias leads us to assume. Finding patterns gives us a sense of control, even if that control comes from mumbo jumbo.

The frequency bias occurs because once we notice an event, especially emotional events, we are hyperaware of repetition. Parents of new babies see infants and pregnant women everywhere and may assume the birth rate has increased or that more young families are moving into the neighborhood. Workers who lose their job think a job massacre is underway. After the market crash in the early 2000s, investors and media became obsessed with volatility, watching for another crash just around the bend even though the next four years were average. The frequency bias can cause marketing planners to discount the role of chance. Marketers who have experienced three or four successes for a particular campaign direction may assume there has been a long-term shift in the trend. Maybe.

The frequency bias is related to the clustering effect (sometimes referred to as the Gambler's fallacy), which sees short-term patterns and assumes the patterns are predictive. The folklore assumption that things happen in threes[9] (e.g., catastrophes, celebrity deaths) is one example. The clustering effect causes people to assume that a heads coin flip is "due" after a string of tails even though the probability of heads is 50–50 every time.

To overcome or avoid this bias, you'll need to accept that in the market's complex system, you'll be better prepared if you assume that tomorrow will be different from today—at least a little.

TAKE THIS AWAY

Marketing plans and subsequent measurement of those plans are essential for coordinating and guiding the actions of a marketing organization. To make plans more successful given the complex market, leaders should shift away from the traditional view of markets as stable places marketing's success can be scored against detailed advance plans and toward a navigator's realm where the marketing plan and the interpretation of scores must be continually adapted. With this transformation, companies will improve the accuracy and reliability of their plans, as well as avoid obstacles. The navigator's mindset will increase marketing's agility and improve market system health.

Actions you can take to become more like a navigator include the following:

1. **Iterate your plans.** Adopt a wayfinding approach that emphasizes continual learning and repeated adaptations.

2. **Think in varying time scales.** Allocate the diverse elements of your plans into a frequency appropriate for the rate of change they need rather than stuffing all planning into an annual cadence that is too frequent for some elements and too slow for others.

3. **Seek feedback.** Gather feedback from multiple sources to inform every level of your plan from long-term strategy to minute-by-minute interactions.

4. **Don't get attached to precise outcomes.** Natural variations in markets mean that outcomes are bound to vary also.

5. Become aware of when the cognitive biases (**normalcy bias** and **frequency bias**) may be distorting planning decisions.

CHAPTER 5

THINK LIKE A STATISTICIAN: FROM SEEKING CERTAINTY TO ACCEPTING PROBABILITY

Chance is always powerful. Let your hook be always cast;
in the pool where you least expect it, there will be a fish.

—**Ovid,** *Heroides*

O utcomes in complex markets do have causes, but they are never the clear reasons our brains crave. The third mind shift toward ComplexityWise marketing encourages managers to avoid seeking a sure thing when making decisions. Instead, they must accept that everything in marketing results from a confluence of several factors and any cause that we consider when making decisions has only a probability of being right. In this chapter, I talk about why chasing certainty leads to futility and frustration in marketing's VUCA world and recommend five mindsets that will help you adopt a statistician's way of thinking.

The inspiration for this mind shift comes from the professionals whose work is invaluable in fields including business, healthcare, government, and many kinds of science, where uncertainty is a fact of life. Thinking like a statistician is difficult for almost everyone because human brains don't naturally think in probabilities. Quite the opposite: We deeply desire our simplified cause-and-effect stories. Uncertainty causes our brains to itch, and only definitive causality seems to be able to adequately scratch it.

Allow me to share a story to illustrate the challenge companies face trying to find reasons for marketing and sales outcomes:

The executive planning meeting wasn't going well. At first, there was good news: Product performance outpaced the competition and several delighted reference customers and market research analysts had given the new product a thumbs up. Then the bad news emerged: Sales weren't growing. What was going wrong?

Managers proposed causes for slow growth, among them the sales leader's claim that marketing leads weren't properly vetted. While admitting to an abundance of prospect interest, he protested, "Plenty of teenagers want to drive a Ferrari, but how many can buy one?" Based on this logic, the group quickly settled on poor lead qualification as the cause of slow growth. On the spot, the CEO decided to divert some marketing budget to hiring an engineer (reporting to sales) to better qualify prospects.

Disappointed and frustrated, the marketing team convened afterward. What was the probability that slow growth for a new product could be attributed to a single cause? It didn't make sense. A deep dive into the sales data revealed something interesting. Out of the dozens of salespeople approved to sell the new product, only an elite handful had ever closed a deal. With this new information, the company executives changed their mind and decided to invest in sales training, rather than prospect qualification. Training helped.

Soon the company found another reason for slow growth. Customers were ill-prepared to make the necessary internal transformations to gain the innovation's benefits. The company began to build a stronger service network to assist transitioning customers. Time uncovered more contributing factors, which the company addressed, and eventually growth accelerated.

This company's leaders initially exhibited behavior that is all too common: jumping on the first reasonable explanation that is proposed. Stuck in the outmoded mindset of seeking certainty, they didn't bother to look around for other—and likely multiple—causes for the lack of product sales. In this chapter, I talk more about this certainty mindset and show why a shift to thinking more in statistical probabilities is a better way to approach marketing today.

HOW A CERTAINTY ORIENTATION IGNORES MARKETING'S REALITIES

Causality explains the relationship between two things: the *effect* (outcome) and the *cause* (factors leading to the effect). Even the smallest children can draw simple conclusions. They understand that the dog ran into the street because someone left the door open. Investigating a chain of events helps us identify and organize the contributing factors that lead to results. But we need one more step; we must identify why the door was left open to determine what to do about it.

Problems arise when decision-makers in complex environments misunderstand the relationship between outcomes and their causes. Simple outcomes, such as why the dog got out, likely result from the sum of a few knowable reasons:

(A) Mom asked Jack to bring in the groceries +
(B) Jack left the door open during this chore +
(C) The dog loves to be outside = the dog got out

This reductionist thought process assumes that all results can be traced back to a chain of understandable causes. And sometimes they can, but reductionism leads to poor decisions in complex environments like consumer markets for the following reasons:

- **Causes aren't completely discoverable.** In complex systems, some information will inevitably be missing. As the company with the innovative product learned, more contributing factors to slow sales were unearthed as they investigated. It was like peeling an onion.

- **Causes aren't always linear.** While some causes in a complex system can be readily and recently linked to an outcome, others are likely to have been set in motion long before and are only now having an effect. For example, when customers made certain relatively small technology choices years ago, those early decisions now create a significant barrier to their adoption.

- **Causes have varying impact.** Some causal factors carry more weight than others, and some factors will diminish or amplify others.

Statistical analysis can tease out insights. With the right analytics, marketers can, for example, identify the 20 percent of known factors that best correlate with business outcomes. With the right analytics, marketers might find that improvements in social sentiment correlate with an increase in closed deals nine months hence or that initiating a new pay-per-click (PPC) campaign correlates with higher web sales.

But correlation, famously, must not be confused with causation. Correlation indicates that two (or more) factors change in seemingly interrelated ways, but it doesn't tell us why the relationships exist. For instance, a child's improved reading ability will correlate with height, but height doesn't cause reading advancement. A third factor, age, contributes to both changes. In some cases of correlation, the relationships are random. Spurious examples abound: One fun use of this faulty thinking is Buzzfeed entertaining readers with silly relationships such as how the average global temperature correlates to the decrease in the number of pirates.

WHY A PROBABILITY ORIENTATION WORKS BETTER

Probability is the mathematical expression of the likelihood of an outcome. Probability can be difficult to understand. It's vague in the way that notions like beauty or love are. Yet, we all have a sense of what probability is. It is the degree to which we believe something to be true. It's a scale of trust ranging from 0 percent to 100 percent. We have a high degree of trust in the probability that the sun will rise tomorrow morning. We have a low degree of trust that the sun will be blue. And somewhere in the middle is the probability of what tomorrow's weather will be.

Probabilities drive decisions. If we believe with 90 percent certainty that tomorrow's weather will be rain, we bring an umbrella. A 10 percent chance of rain means leave it at home. Marketing outcomes exist somewhere in the middle of that scale of trust. Like weather, marketing is semipredictable. Companies make very different decisions about the launch strategy for an innovative new product if they are 20 percent certain they've got a viable market versus being 80 percent certain. Probability plays a role in forecasting (anticipating conditions), in retrospectives (looking back at what happened), and in evaluations (judging the quality, importance, or amount of something).

In one way, a statistician's mindset is simply accepting the world will always have two components: certainty (I'm 60 percent confident that this campaign will bring in at least $20,000 in revenue) and uncertainty (the remaining 40 percent represents trusting that a better or worse outcome could occur). See figure 5.1.

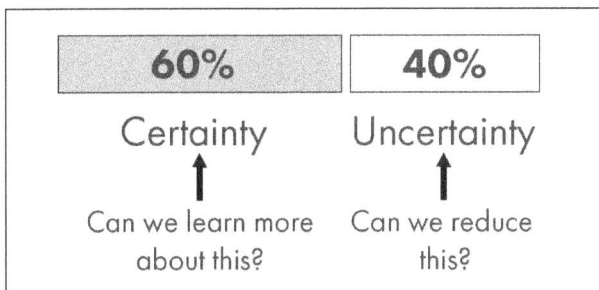

Figure 5.1: Considering Both Sides of Probability

Information seeking reduces uncertainty. However, each information-seeking task has a cost, and decision-makers must consider how much certainty is needed. It would be great if applying time and money could finally reduce all uncertainty, but in complex situations, nothing can reduce the uncertainty gap to zero, regardless of the stakes.

HOW TO THINK LIKE A STATISTICIAN

There are four mindsets that will help you think more like a statistician and become more comfortable dealing with uncertainty:

1. Make peace with not knowing

2. Place bets

3. Broaden your sources of information

4. Seek clarity where ambiguity exists

In this section, I explain what each of these mindsets means and how they contribute to thinking more like a statistician.

Make Peace with Not Knowing

Except under a limited number of circumstances, executives seeking high degrees of certainty in marketing decisions are guaranteed disappointment. Outcome certainty depends on the number of influential factors, how powerful these factors are, and the amount of time lag that allows for interactions to produce confounding feedback.

Because marketing (and sales) outcomes depend on how humans behave as individuals and in groups, we can look to the social sciences (e.g., economics, psychology, sociology, anthropology, political science) for the range of certainty to expect. In the social sciences, high levels of certainty, such as the 90–95 percent confidence levels seen in university statistics classes, are unusual. An inspection of 708 studies from the cognitive and behavioral sciences found that only 3 percent resulted in correlations of .50 or greater[1] between a given cause and an outcome. Any correlation greater than .50 is considered strong. What we can conclude from this finding is that hardly any single factor in marketing (e.g., campaigns, competitor actions, pricing changes, etc.) will *by itself* predictably move the needle. There are no magic bullets, no one or two things that if you do these alone, sales will be guaranteed. There are no coins you can put into the vending machine and reliably out pops your treat.

Rather than being like addition of simple factors (A + B + C = Result), marketing is like algebra, where the factors that create the result have more complicated relationships: X(a) + Y(b) + Z(c) = Result. With enough data and experimentation, companies should be able to find *combinations* of elements that improve the chances of favorable outcomes, and some of those elements will be under company control. For example, a company might find that one method, let's say improving search engine optimization, makes the highest contribution to good sales outcomes. However, other tactics must also be in play. Appear early in search results, *and* make sure that social media sentiment is high, *and* ensure happy referral customers.

Place Bets

Ask a fan of a beleaguered baseball team who they want to win the World Series, and they will absolutely name their favorite team. Now ask them to *bet* on who will win, to put some skin in the game, and you'll get a different answer. When something valuable is at stake, we bet on how we believe the world works, not wishful thinking. How confident are you (really) in your marketing strategy? Forty percent? Sixty percent? How much would you be willing to bet?

Betting puts a price on beliefs. Decision-scientist and former professional poker player Annie Duke offers betting as an antidote for mental traps. Poker, like marketing, involves making risky decisions despite incomplete, hidden information. Assigning a probability to a decision reflects our understanding that information will always be incomplete and that luck plays a significant role in outcomes. Poker players can encounter twenty decisions per hand, says Duke, making the competition a useful lab. John von Neumann,[2] whose work revolutionized economics, modeled his game theories on a stripped-down version of poker.

Money is the most familiar currency for betting. In a way, allocating the marketing budget is a bet on marketing returns. In business, accountability to outcomes can also be a currency for bets. It's one thing to blab opinions if there are no repercussions for being wrong. It's another to justify that decision to others. Accountability encourages open-mindedness because it nudges us toward the acceptance of new information. It drives us to be vigilant about the accuracy of our beliefs and makes us more likely to vet our beliefs rather than simply assuming we are right. If rewards increase because of greater decision certainty, then we can feel smart about improving the odds—even if the reality is that sometimes luck wrenches the outcome.

THE BEST FORECASTERS LOVE BASE RATES

Superforecasters[TM3] consistently predict more accurately than average people and often better than experts using techniques that don't always rely on sophisticated statistics. In *Superforecasting: The Art and Science of Prediction*, the authors highlight a key skill: applying *base rates*, defined as the percentage of a population sharing a characteristic.

Use of base rates helps avoid the common mental habit of prioritizing vivid experiences over dull facts and is more valuable when multiple factors are considered. For example, to determine whether Kenneth, who is highly creative, is a salesperson or a marketer, one might think, "Marketers are often creative people, so if Kenneth is creative, then I estimate there to be a 60 percent chance that he is a marketer." Superforecasters, however, break down the prediction to first consider an essential base rate. With roughly three marketers for every ninety-seven salespeople in the US[4] in 2023, and assuming all marketers are creative while only 10 percent of salespeople are, the odds of Kenneth being a marketer drop to just 20 percent.

Broaden Your Sources of Information

Put in mathematical terms, to improve confidence in the face of uncertainty you need to identify the right combination of factors that collectively will produce an algorithm with the best fit to the outcome. "Best fit" means you minimize both the number of times your predictions are wrong and the amount of your error.

Your chances of arriving at the most accurate array of causes improves if you seek data and information from diverse sources. Diverse viewpoints are checks on fallibility because they bring in a broader set of private information. James Surowiecki, in his classic book *The Wisdom of Crowds*,[5] describes how everyone forms unique viewpoints based on what everyone knows (*public information*) plus what only they know (*private information*). Private information is a term used by economists to represent the aggregate of concrete data, interpretation, analysis, and intuition gathered by an individual. When the group of information sources is truly diverse, then each person's view, says Surowiecki, will be somewhat right and somewhat wrong, but each will be wrong in different ways, and these various forms of wrongness cancel each other out while the rightness will be reinforced.

Suppose you have only 30 percent confidence in your company's ability to succeed in a new market because you understand existing resource constraints. If you independently query eight savvy people with a variety of experiences, chances are a couple will see the situation the way you do, while the others possess private information about market conditions, customer attitudes, and product competitiveness that could raise your confidence level to 80 percent—or bring it to zero. With the addition of each view, the opportunity to reduce uncertainty increases, provided that the aggregation meets appropriate conditions.

Groupthink[6] becomes an issue when your sources of information are primarily from those who share your world view and much of their public and private information on a topic is similar to yours. This is a frequent problem among work groups who have been together for years. It's also a problem when marketing only uses marketing-produced data to look for answers rather than seeking insight from other company groups and external sources. On the positive side of homogeneous working groups, they are more cohesive and easier to manage. However, the members tend to be more insulated from outside opinion and more convinced their small group is right. Groupthink works not by censoring but by making dissent improbable. Dissent seems to disappear along with doubt. Common mindsets and data sources mean that the members will rationalize away disagreement, and it's easier for a dissenter to change their mind than challenge the group.

In the 1950s, the Rand Corporation developed the Delphi method of building consensus. A facilitator asks participants to privately submit estimates (or votes or answers to questionnaires) on a topic. Between each of several rounds, the facilitator shares the answers with the participants and invites them to think again. This process continues until the group ends up with a judged consensus.

One reason the Delphi method works is that all participants remain anonymous to each other. If new information is collected independently, errors are less likely to replicate. On the other hand, groups who observe each other before deciding can suffer from *confirmatory drift*, meaning that over time they become more alike in their thinking. People start to value public information (what they see others doing) over their private information (what they think is right). Social influence reduces group diversity without diminishing collective error.

Leaders must not only seek diverse, independent sources to augment their own information but also foster and defend contrarians. Although everyone hates short sellers in the stock market (those who trade on gloom), they are valuable error correctors. Better decisions are reached if each member of a group seeks their own private information and then pools.

Seek Clarity Where Ambiguity Exists

To achieve quality decisions, it's also useful to increase precision in the information you use. You have a high degree of precision if several reasonable people with the same information reach the same conclusion, sort of like a jury. But when a decision is a judgment, it's difficult to be precise because judgments have no exact rules for contributors to refer to. Examples of judgments in marketing management include determining brand values, setting offering prices, choosing a particular agency, and deciding whether to promote someone. When we make judgments, we use a mental measurement scale not necessarily numerical. Although marketing decisions will never be black and white, you don't want to add to complexity by having decision-makers all comparing choices to random mental models. You will make better decisions if you can get the decision-making group closer to agreeing on definitions. Unresolved differences in opinion or taste matter little and can cause serious problems.

If judgment outcomes are verifiable, in other words later able to be checked and demonstrated to be true, developing a scale helps cut through ambiguity. Harvard psychologist Stanley Smith Stevens, an expert on measurement in social systems, discovered that even a single intermediate anchor (called a *modulus*) helps with clarifying decisions. Scales and benchmarks increase realism and fairness and help avoid blind spots.

Optimal scales will exhibit clear upper and lower boundaries and include fact-based benchmarks in between. I once worked with a company that needed to rationalize marketing expenses in regional offices. The requested budgets were all over the board. The scale we came up with calculated the ratio of marketing investment to revenue in each office to create the range. Then, combining a few metrics, including sales productivity, customer loyalty, and market opportunity size, we selected the six top-performing offices. The average marketing budget for this collection was set as a benchmark. These three data points helped the leadership team determine how to allocate budget. Judgment was still needed—should each office be higher or lower than the benchmark and why. But it took the decision out of the random opinion category and into sanity.

The goal is not to stamp out randomness, which is not only impossible but also not ideal. The organic world needs some variation and stress to survive. We like games, mysteries, and horror films. A healthy heart has a little variation in the beat. However, getting closer to the statistician's math and reducing ambiguity where it adds no value improves decisions in the complex marketing world.

COGNITIVE BIASES THAT INTERFERE WITH STATISTICAL THINKING

If you desire to think like a statistician, it will be helpful to be aware of three universal cognitive biases—the fundamental attribution error, hindsight bias, and confirmation bias—that can lead decision-makers down faulty paths as to the causes of outcomes.

Fundamental Attribution Error ("It's not my fault")—Every outcome culminates from a combination of skill (internal factors we can influence) and luck (external factors out of our control). The fundamental attribution error is one of the most dangerous biases because it misleads us into incorrectly attributing which is which. Confusing skill and luck blocks managers from seeing opportunities to learn and course correct.

Here's the bias: In an unconscious effort to make ourselves look good and feel safe, we overly attribute positive outcomes to our skill ("our campaign was very creative") while downplaying the role of luck ("the competitor's product was late to market"). We take the opposite stance with negative outcomes, overweighting the role of external factors ("I couldn't meet the deadline because sales operations didn't give me the data in time") compared to factors we could have done something about ("I wasn't timely in my request"). Periods with good outcomes, such as several quarters of revenue growth, lead managers to believe they've made clever decisions. Negative periods are blamed on circumstances, when management decisions may have had something to do with it.

Tips for fighting this bias come from Annie Duke, author of *Thinking in Bets: Making Smarter Decisions When You Don't Have All the Facts,*[7] who suggests a method of distinguishing between the two:

- Call it *skill* if making the same decision again would conclusively drive the same outcome or if making a different decision would result in a different outcome. Skill plays a dominant role in a chess game victory because chess has many rules, moves are calculated, and there are few outside influences. Companies would love for marketing outcomes to be mostly attributable to skill so it could deliver vending machine–type results most of the time.

- Duke says we should designate to the *luck* category any other contributing uncontrollable or unforeseeable factors (e.g., other people's actions, the weather, a change in the competitive landscape, randomness, hidden events). Because of the VUCA nature of marketing, outcomes contain a significant portion of luck.

Hindsight Bias ("We should have known")—Hindsight bias is our tendency to assume that once an outcome is known, it was inevitable. This bias leads us to erroneously believe that all causes for an outcome are identifiable *if only* we (or they) were smarter, had more data, or spent more time. With the extra knowledge, we would have done something different and *then* a positive outcome would have occurred. Hindsight bias leads us to assume that poor outcomes must have been produced by bad decisions and great outcomes by brilliant ones.

To deal with hindsight bias, understand that complexity *guarantees* a significant number of unknowns, so we can't know everything in advance, nor can others. At best, we can expect partial foresight. Because of so much hidden information, both good and poor outcomes should be viewed as signals to be investigated rather than as judgments of inevitability.

Confirmation Bias ("See! I knew it!")—Although we like to consider ourselves as open-minded, humans unconsciously look for evidence to confirm what we already believe. We pay attention to and give more credence to information that supports us while discounting or rejecting information that opposes.

I witnessed confirmation bias during a marketing leadership meeting at a global software company. An analyst presented compelling evidence that one of the company's primary market segments had saturated, thus risking future revenue. She presented three alternative markets where growth was more promising. I expected the marketing leadership team to discuss the situation or, at a minimum, acknowledge it and table the topic for later review. Instead, after a period of silence, the field marketing leader said, "That doesn't jive with my experience." He proceeded to detail a story about a new customer in China. I was astonished. No questions were asked. No comments made. The CMO thanked the analyst and moved to the next agenda item, a lively discussion of the new brand campaign.

While it's impossible to know what was going on in the heads of the marketing VPs at that table, I can imagine the anxiety that influenced their confirmation bias. All their case studies, references, social networks, ads, and sales territories buttressed the existing market. Initiating a new vertical market would be a huge undertaking. Should they even believe the market analysis? Much information is just noise. *The New York Times*[8] reported in 2009 that the average American consumed thirty-four gigabytes of information each day and one hundred thousand words a day crossed our eyes and ears, more than twice the size of *War and Peace*. The marketing leadership team was right to be cautious.

But the analyst's report was no superfluous Instagram feed. Ignoring her report foreshadowed real problems for the company, and later, the marketing leaders were criticized for not paying attention to it when it was first presented. On the other hand, the VP of field marketing's story was just an anecdote, but one that confirmed tradition. The marketing leadership team wanted to believe the story, not the facts.

Our ability for self-deception knows few bounds. We prefer consistency over logic. We'd rather believe the story that is most coherent, the one that makes sense with our world view (especially if it makes us look good or calms our fears). To counteract confirmation bias, train yourself to distinguish between plausibility (the story that makes sense) and probability (the likelihood that the story is true).

TAKE THIS AWAY

Marketing leaders make hundreds of decisions that affect their company's agility and market system health. ComplexityWise marketing advocates for shifting away from seeking definitive causes for marketing outcomes (good or bad) and toward accepting that outcomes derive multiple contributing factors, any of which have a probability of happening. With a statistician's mindset, companies will improve the quality of marketing decisions leading to better outcomes.

To become more like a statistician, do the following:

1. **Make peace with not knowing.** Marketing outcomes depend on the number of influential factors, and while using appropriate analytical and decision methods will improve the accuracy of attribution, some things will never be known, and that must be okay.

2. **Place bets.** Betting puts a price on beliefs. Marketing involves making risky decisions despite incomplete, hidden information. Assigning a probability to a decision reflects our understanding

that information will always be incomplete and that luck plays a significant role in outcomes.

3. **Broaden your sources of information.** Diversifying the data on which decisions are made improves the accuracy of those decisions.

4. **Clarify ambiguity.** Improve the precision of decision-making by using clarity tools such as scales and benchmarks.

5. **Reduce the power of cognitive biases.** Become aware of when **fundamental attribution error**, **hindsight bias**, and **confirmation bias** may be playing an inappropriate role in decision-making.

CHAPTER 6

THINK LIKE AN ECOLOGIST: FROM A MECHANIC'S VIEW OF INDIVIDUALS TO CONSIDERING CONTEXT

Many leaders are tempted to lead like a chess master, striving to control every move, when they should be leading like gardeners, creating and maintaining a viable ecosystem in which the organization operates.

—**Stanley A. McChrystal,** *Team of Teams: New Rules of Engagement for a Complex World*

When I began working on the topic of marketing management in a VUCA world, I focused on the debate surrounding marketing ROI. This led me to the first three mind shifts, Think Like an Investor, Think Like a Navigator, and Think Like a Statistician, as well as many of the practices that I discuss in part III. As I got deeper into how marketing as a system works, I realized that the transformation to ComplexityWise marketing will be incapacitated if marketing leaders don't also shift their thinking about people management. The people piece is unquestionably challenging. However, dodging it would be like missing a chair leg. No matter how strong the other legs, the chair is bound to collapse.

The literature about organizational systems thinking is filled with comparisons of leadership models. Out with mechanistic, command-and-control approaches and in with those that are more humane and naturalistic. Marketing leaders will be familiar with many aspects of this management evolution. Terms such as *servant leaders* and *coaches* have been used for a while. The shift toward ComplexityWise marketing goes further than progressing leadership style, and even exemplary leaders have something to learn.

Early systems expert Peter Senge said, "The most universal challenge that we face is the transition from seeing our human institutions as machines to seeing them as embodiments of nature . . . We keep bringing in mechanics—when what we need are gardeners."[1] General Stanley McChrystal also suggests "gardener" as an alternative to the chess master archetype embedded in many leaders' psyche. I like the term *ecologist*, which, although related to gardener, evokes a fresh attention to the organizational ecosystem.

Which leads me to the fourth mind shift required for managing marketing in a complex, variable world: Stop the mechanic's reductive perspective that thinks of employees solely as individuals removed from their context, and stop the chess master's assumption that it is leaders who direct the organization's behavior and performance. The former leaves an amazing opportunity on the table, and the latter is just an illusion.

Instead, think like an ecologist who respects the environment, understanding that someone's behavior—which drives performance—emerges at the *intersection* of the individual and their context (e.g., social, cultural, economic). The metaphor of ecologist awakens a vibrant image of the organization as part of a natural world. It connotes growth, connection, and integration. Rather than studying plants or animals in labs, naturalists increasingly consider organisms within their habitat as they have learned that in an ecosystem everything is connected to everything else.

Leaders are part of this context, but not the most influential part. In this chapter, I explain more about how this intersection of individual and context works along with the implications, and I share four mindsets that will help you adopt an ecologist's way of thinking.

HOW A MECHANIC'S ORIENTATION FAILS PEOPLE

Leaders who think like mechanics see themselves as architects, builders, and fixers. It's a top-down, directive approach, even if the leaders are kind and empathetic. Leader-mechanics aren't necessarily bad people. A master mechanic is talented, experienced, and works hard to improve their skills and results. They value the tools of their trade and try to take good care of them. However, organizations are not machines, and viewing people as discrete components whose talents you use to get stuff done can lead to disadvantage.

At a minimum, the mechanic's reductive perspective leads even otherwise exceptional managers to leave a powerful feature of complex systems on the table, that is, the advantage of connection. As I discuss earlier, most of the power in a system works through the interactions and feedback occurring outside of our purview. Beyond that oversight, managers who also neglect how important people are to success in a VUCA economy risk losing a primary source of value. Employees are not simply labor-producing tools. In a VUCA world, enterprises will succeed through innovation, problem-solving, and relationships, rather than simply controlling production. Therefore, companies who best harness people's potential will be the most successful. The more VUCA the environment, as in marketing, the truer this is. It's reported that Bill Gates, former CEO and chairman of Microsoft, once said, "The inventory, the value of my company, walks out the door every evening."

At the far extreme of the mechanic's viewpoint are the few managers who are truly users, hardly considering the people aspect at all. Stories about these low-grade villains who subjugate workers in their greedy, self-centered quests are rare enough to make sensational headlines and streaming video content. Fortunately, I've never met or even heard of a marketing leader who comes close to this egregious state. I mention it here only to point out how injurious this perspective gets.

Although the mechanics mindset has been around for more than a century, it reached a peak during the 1990s with the prevalence of the aptly named Business Process Reengineering (BPR) model. Introduced by the also aptly named Michael Hammer, who wrote the #1 best-selling business book of its time, *Reengineering the Corporation*,[2] BPR's appeal hinged on the promise of an aggressive and speedy resolution to the challenge of rising global competition. Starting with a clean sheet of paper, BPR's proponents scorched the current business state and then attempted to build an ideal future state in the cleared space. This Tayloresque solution became known in some circles as "rip and replace."

Within a few years of lamentable attempts, it became clear that real transformation was rarely achieved, and the only consistent outcome was reduced headcount associated with large numbers of traumatized employees. Hammer later admitted with dismay to *The Wall Street Journal*, "I wasn't smart enough about that. I was reflecting my engineering background and was insufficiently appreciative of the human dimension. I've learned that's critical."[3] Ironically, the BPR model hasn't died out. The book has been reprinted and various revised models continue to be used.

WHY AN ECOLOGIST'S ORIENTATION WORKS BETTER

The leader as an ecologist pays attention to individual people, of course, but also tends, nurtures, and guides the organizational habitat to give people the best chance to flourish. Just as companies are effectively organisms within market ecosystems, so marketers are organisms within the greater context of the organizational system.

Healthy ecosystems are alive with a diverse cast of coordinating creatures. The National Geographic Society defines an ecosystem as a "geographic area where plants, animals, and other organisms, as well as weather and landscapes, work together to form a bubble of life."[4] In Northern California where I live, winemakers know that vineyards consist of the grape vines, of course. Yeasts, fungi, and bacteria also profoundly influence vine health and produce "terroir," a wine's distinctive regional characteristics. Insects and a variety of grasses, cereals, or legumes add to the ecosystem mix, as does sunlight, water, human workers, and even pollution from nearby road traffic. The latter is a reminder that not everything in an ecosystem is good.

The organizational ecosystem is made up of tangible elements, not only people but also information technology and other equipment, as well as things like the offices where people work. Intangible elements are also part of the system, including things like reward systems, codes of conduct, job descriptions, and the company's reputation.

To help the ecosystem and its member organisms thrive, the ecologist *cultivates conditions for success*. In a vineyard, for example, the vines need water, soil, light, and fertilizer. Good wine-grape growers provide trellises to support optimal growth. Thinking like an ecologist means tending to the environment as a whole is more effective than micro-controlling individual plants. Anyone who has done any gardening understands you can't command a vine, a tomato, or a fern to grow. There is an African proverb that gently reminds, "Grass does not grow faster if you pull it." Plants grow by themselves just as people can and do develop on their own if given the right environment.

I learned a lesson about the importance of organizational context when a large company engaged me to guide their marketing department toward the capabilities critically needed to deliver their future strategy. The company had made several acquisitions to bring in cutting-edge products and talent. C-suite executives said all the right things. The vision was intelligent, crystal clear, and well communicated. Yet, marketing remained stuck in the old ways. Interviews with middle-managers revealed a horrifying story. Behind the scenes, managers who had been at the company for a long time were bullying and undermining the newly arrived marketers' attempts to utilize their fresh ideas and skills. Although senior leaders were astonished and dismayed at this situation, this awareness spurred them to make some changes to the environment such as initiating extra training, coaching, and change support for legacy employees and proactively doing more to assist new marketers to team up and adjust.

The ecologist's mindset is relatively nascent in business, and the business processes in most companies haven't caught up. Consider the people management processes in your company. Do they almost exclusively focus on the individual only? Do new people get hired to fill a particular job with little attention to the team they will join? Beyond a little onboarding, is there any formal effort to help them fit in and collaborate? Is compensation based on individual responsibility and performance? Do managers evaluate singular employees' strengths and weaknesses? If things don't work out, is the individual employee the first and sometimes only place where intervention takes place? If downsizing or reorganization is necessary, does anyone address the impact on the organizational community?

HOW TO THINK LIKE AN ECOLOGIST

Four mindsets play an important role in beginning to think like an organizational ecologist:

1. Prioritize culture

2. Be a role model

3. Nurture the network

4. Rethink internal competition

In this section, I talk about each of these mindsets and show how they contribute to an ecological, system focus.

Prioritize Culture

The ecologist-leader's playbook should be about influencing culture. Culture is the organization's longest time layer. It exerts the strongest influence on behavior and thus offers the best insurance for reliable and scalable agility. As shown in figure 6.1, changing marketing's operational tool set is easier and quicker but far less powerful than changing its culture. You might think about technology and processes as analogous to the short-term-oriented demand generation with culture acting like the long-term strategy of brand building.

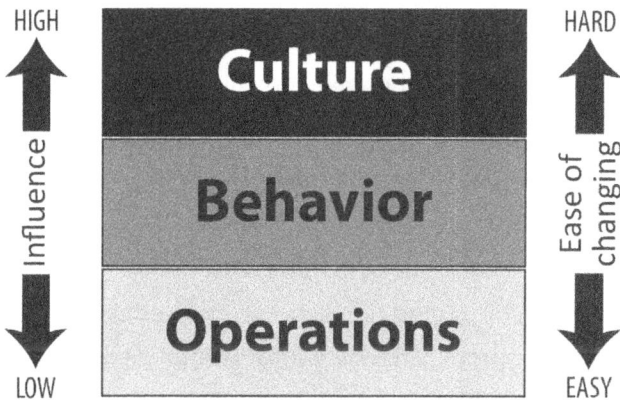

Figure 6.1: The Influence of Culture

Culture consists of the ways things get done, saturated with the meaning that people ascribe to those actions. Every organization directs behavior via formal artifacts, including policies, instructions, and protocols. These matter, but these are dwarfed by the hidden influence factors. "Culture comprises the unwritten rules that guide people every day. Not the policy manuals or the organization charts that depict how things are supposed to get done in an imaginary world," write the authors of *The Future-Proof Workplace*.[5] Culture is social. It works like a magnet, pulling people into its center. The most ideal operational practices will not compensate if there exists a culture that tugs individuals off course.

An example of these unwritten rules is expressed by this story from a senior leader from a famous Silicon Valley company who transferred to the California headquarters from the London office. Upon arrival, a human resources executive told him that the California office had no dress code policy and therefore the executive was free to dress as he liked. So, the man continued to wear the formal clothes he had enjoyed in the UK—a dress shirt, cufflinks, and gray flannel pants. After repeated reminders about no dress code policy, he finally realized that there was indeed a dress code in Silicon Valley; it just wasn't overtly expressed. To fit into the Valley culture, people were expected to dress informally.

Although it can't be worked on directly, culture is going to arise, so leaders may as well try to shape it. Practices, rituals, and language consistent with the desired culture must be encouraged as they emerge from the organization. Fledgling practices must be protected from the crush of the existing industrial-era valence. Since much of what happens in a system comes from activity hidden from observation, leaders can be blindsided by what is happening out of their purview. Leaders must monitor progress to diagnose illness and nip it in the bud.

To thrive in a VUCA environment, here are five cultural attributes that you should focus on developing in your organization:

- **Continuous learning:** Perpetual scanning for what's changed and incorporating new information enhances people's ability to adapt. Leaders cultivate a learning culture by investing in the skills and tools for asking questions, listening, collecting information, analysis, and decision-making. Mistakes become opportunities for learning.

- **Equanimity:** Uncertainty can produce feelings of confusion, ambiguity, and fear. The ability to manage one's emotions is essential for working in complex environments. Equanimity is a state where we feel challenging emotions but don't get tangled up in them. Buddhist scholar Peter Harvey described equanimity as the "stirred not shaken," the opposite of James Bond's martini, "shaken not stirred." Leaders can encourage "sandboxes," which are places where people can practice equanimity by doing new (and scary) things in a safe place. Salespeople frequently get this kind of training but not marketers.

- **Entrepreneurialism:** Although acting thoughtlessly isn't a great strategy, you don't want people stopping when things change fast. In a complex situation, top-down instructions are too slow in arriving. Therefore, leaders need people to be spontaneous volunteers, to courageously step out of their lane to do what is needed. Leaders promote entrepreneurialism through power-sharing, reducing bureaucracy, and honoring those who volunteer to tackle enterprise issues and devote their capability and spirit to important, purposeful projects.

- **Empathy:** ComplexityWise marketing requires customer-centricity and the ability to work in diverse groups. Both require people to develop an appreciation for "the other." Empathy doesn't require that everyone agrees or even accepts other people's views or actions. Empathy is simply an acknowledgment that the other person is a human being worthy of our respect. Empathy practices include respectful listening and trying to tune in to other people's emotions.

- **Trust:** Because ComplexityWise marketing requires greater freedom than industrial-era approaches, a higher degree of trust amongst workers and leaders is needed. Lack of trust is a tax on the enterprise because excess oversight is unwieldy and costly. If people can speak candidly with each other about what they know about the market, the quality of work, and ways to improve things, they increase opportunities for innovation and problem-solving.

Be a Role Model

It's unlikely that new effects introduced into the ecosystem will embed until the organization's leaders visibly personify and champion desired behavior. Culture is a trailing indicator, so how leaders acted in the past infuses today's behavior. Therefore, it's paramount that leaders take literally the meaning of leadership as "one who goes first."

Your organization isn't stupid. In the many organizational change efforts I've participated in, there is often a deep employee skepticism about whether change will stick. By personifying the new way, leaders inspire people to go through the necessary effort for transformation. For instance, if a new strategy calls for increased customer centricity, leaders can make customer satisfaction part of the formal metrics and reward systems (including their own). A leader's language is a subtle but powerful clue to what they really think. Do leaders use or allow combative language when speaking about customers? Do they use terms such as "we need to suck the oxygen out of the room" or the use of war and hunting analogies when talking about customers? Or are more empathetic and collaborative alternatives encouraged?

As they climb the organizational ladders, leaders may forget about the difficulty of barriers their employees face. As experts, leaders want to provide solutions and may fear that asking questions and trying new things will make them look incompetent. I recall one senior executive who stormed out of a team training when it became clear that some of his staff were better at a new skill than he was. Humility is realistic in complex situations and therefore a strength that leaders can model.

Nurture the Network

The organizational ecosystem doesn't end at the departmental edges. It extends far beyond, and leaders must look beyond their immediate reports to the larger group that comprises the organizational network. This means paying attention to relationships not only between their team members but also between those staff and others in the greater ecosystem. The authors of the book *The Future-Proof Workplace* suggest that success "is about getting the right people together to tackle issues no matter where they are in the organization, or who they report to."[6]

Organizational network links come in many shapes and sizes. There are formal and obvious links as well as the informal connections that are largely unseen, powerful, and often forgotten about. There are conversations that happen through private platforms such as Microsoft Teams and Slack and public channels such as LinkedIn, WhatsApp, and TikTok. But most conversations are part of what some people call "dark social" and, therefore, are completely untraceable. Leaders must accept these social conduits are in play and not be surprised, or angered, by them. More about managing links is discussed in chapter 8: The Organization: Integrated Teams.

I learned a lesson about the importance of cross-functional connection when I was brought in to fix a broken marketing operations process requiring departmental coordination. When I arrived, I found a situation typical of serial business processes where one group completes a task and passes it baton-style to the next group. Throughput was slow. Tasks frequently got dropped. People blamed each other, and there was pressure to fire the scapegoat. Upon investigation, I learned that each person in the chain was simply acting locally, making rational decisions based on their own goals, but they all lacked a view of how they fit into the big picture.

To fill this information void, I had the group walk through the process steps with each person describing what they did and why. Almost immediately, mental lights went on. "Oh! Is that what you need? I can easily change my way to get that for you." Many things immediately improved through just this communication, and the group got an even bigger productivity boost when we combined everyone into a virtual team with the power to create a more integrated process. They named themselves and accepted joint accountability for a business metric rather than their previous local goals. The troublemaker ended up being a very competent problem-solver. Over time, the team simplified their process without management intervention. When one person left the company, others voluntarily stepped in to do their work and the team agreed it was unnecessary to replace the missing worker.

Rethink Internal Competition

Competition is a fact of life in every ecosystem. Competition in nature occurs when individuals or species go after the same scarce resources, such as food, mates, or den sites. Humans are hardwired to compete. We will compete for scarce resources as do all organisms. Humans, being social beings, also constantly make social comparisons, where people measure their performance or other attributes with others to see where they stand.

The external competition that transpires between companies in market ecosystem we generally view as positive because it obliges each to become better at what they do. However, internal competition usually isn't beneficial. Complex organizations get work done primarily through coordination not competition, that is working together harmoniously to accomplish something, and through cooperation, which is when people coordinate *voluntarily*, rising to a broader sense of self-interest, while trusting others to do the same. Excessive internal competition erodes cooperation. The way leaders handle the competitive aspect of the ecosystem has an impact on the organization's agility and the ability to compete externally.

Leaders can't stop people from feeling and acting competitively, but they don't need to sponsor this attitude. William P. Barnett, professor of business leadership, strategy, and organizations at the Stanford Graduate School of Business, says, "Competition already exists in your organization. If you turn up the heat and have even more competition than is naturally occurring, you can easily—and almost predictively—spill over into having the maladaptive problems that come from too much competition."[7] Handled poorly, internal competition causes people to be risk averse and fearful of making mistakes. They tend to horde resources. Distrust increases and productivity deteriorates. Internal competition is at the root of many toxic workplaces and is often the cause of marketing vs. sales problems.

Often resources are indeed scarce. Managers must make tough decisions about things like where marketing budgets go, the distribution of annual raises, how to parse the time available for speaking in meetings, and the number of promotional spots. Leaders can make these choices while still keeping in mind that cooperation is paramount. Yet, most companies set up rivalries (inadvertently or on purpose) with individuated practices such as quotas, personal MBOs (Management by Objectives), and rating systems that split people apart rather than pull them together. Niels Pflaeging, author of *Organize for Complexity*, points out in his blog the folly of individual internal competition, explaining that "individual performance, in organizations, does not even exist. Here, performance emerges in the space between people. That is the nature of the organization."[8]

Leaders need to manage competition responsibly. Acknowledge it, understand it, and guide the group to resolution. Help teams recover and reconvene after a difficult situation. Instead of interpreting competition as a battle where only one side wins, it can be reframed as one way to encourage new things that benefit the greater good.

At the same time, leaders can strengthen cooperation. Cooperation requires a degree of reciprocity. Relationship durability contributes to cooperation because people are aware that they will need to work with the same people in the future and payback will occur. Leaders can further encourage cooperation by monitoring fairness practices and negotiation and by power sharing and bridge building.

A COGNITIVE BIAS THAT INTERFERES WITH ECOLOGICAL THINKING

To think like an ecologist, marketing leaders will find it helpful to be alert to their tendency and that of their team to default to the *representative bias*, which leads us to ascribe reasons or motives based on stereotypes ("Oh, she's like *that*").

Managing in an organizational ecosystem containing a multitude of people with broad and varied attributes requires that leaders stretch their understanding of others. Healthy coral reefs support a vast array of marine life—sea anemones, fish, sponges, turtles—and experts on one or two aquatic species can't presume they know others.

While humans share more attributes than say, a clown fish and an octopus, marketing leaders ought not assume that because they understand marketers, they therefore get salespeople, finance pros, and data analysts. Intuitively, we know this. But we all harbor mental prototypes of others that serve as cognitive shortcuts. The representative bias leads us to unconsciously apply those mental prototypes to whole groups.

The term stereotype suggests characteristics such as race, gender, and age. Modern managers know to watch out for these. But what about the stereotypes that people hold about occupational roles? A few of the stereotypes I've encountered from marketers include the following:

- Salespeople are "coin operated" and care only about themselves

- CEOs care only about money

- Customer service reps are impersonal

- CFOs are "bean counters" and not strategic

- Software developers are poor socializers

Stereotypes are simplified versions of rich knowledge structures partially based on our personal experience and are, thus, difficult to dislodge. Leaders may even hold assumptions about marketing practitioners, such as marketers don't know much about math. One theory[9] suggests that stereotypes form when we observe a trait that seems overrepresented in a group, such as women are caregivers, and then generalize that trait to the whole group.

The representative bias interferes with a leader's ability to think about the variability in the organizational ecosystem and to help their team break out of old thinking and preconceived ideas of what's possible. Under the sway of the representative bias, leaders have blind spots about people's real needs and may neglect to provide the right kinds of contextual support for performance.

The good news is that exposure to alternative models helps crumble unconscious prototypes. As the saying goes, "You have to see it before you can be it." Identifying exemplary behaviors, for example, holding up a math-adept marketer and an empathetic salesperson as local heroes, provides people with new data for their mental models and nudges thinking in a more expansive and productive direction.

TAKE THIS AWAY

Since the wake-up call of the harsh 1990s, more humane (and effective) management frameworks have been adopted by most marketing leaders. Regardless of the quality of the framework or the leader's good intentions, marketing challenges will persist if leaders continue to apply them with a mechanic's frame of mind. We don't work in a completely knowable world, and therefore leaders can't make the business machine work by rationally laying out plans and issuing clear directions to individual employees. More is needed—and available.

Marketing leaders as ecologists respect the organizational environment, understanding that everyone's behavior, including their own, emerges at the intersection of the individual and their context. They must shift away from the conventional reductive perspective that individuals are like components of a machine and can be treated separately from each other and from everything else. Leaders, no matter how well qualified, aren't master mechanics directing the organization's behavior and performance. They are very important participants in the ecosystem, but it's the organization—as a whole—that wields the greatest power, and they will get best results by cultivating the holistic environment.

Here are actions you can take to do that:

1. **Prioritize culture:** Culture exerts the strongest influence on behavior and thus offers the best insurance for reliable and scalable change. Foster the cultural attributes that will help the marketing organization perform best in the VUCA environment.

2. **Be a role model:** It's paramount that leaders take literally the meaning of leadership as "one who goes first." By personifying new ways, leaders inspire people to go through the necessary effort for transformation.

3. **Nurture the network:** In complex systems where connectivity is the superpower, leaders must look beyond their immediate reports to the larger group, fostering connections that will unleash the ecosystems power.

4. **Rethink internal competition:** While competition is an inevitable feature of an organizational ecosystem, it can erode essential cooperation. Leaders must take care to manage competition wisely and not to feed the flames.

5. **Reduce the power of representative bias:** Become aware of the tendency to default to the representative heuristic, and work to expand knowledge of the variety of attributes in others.

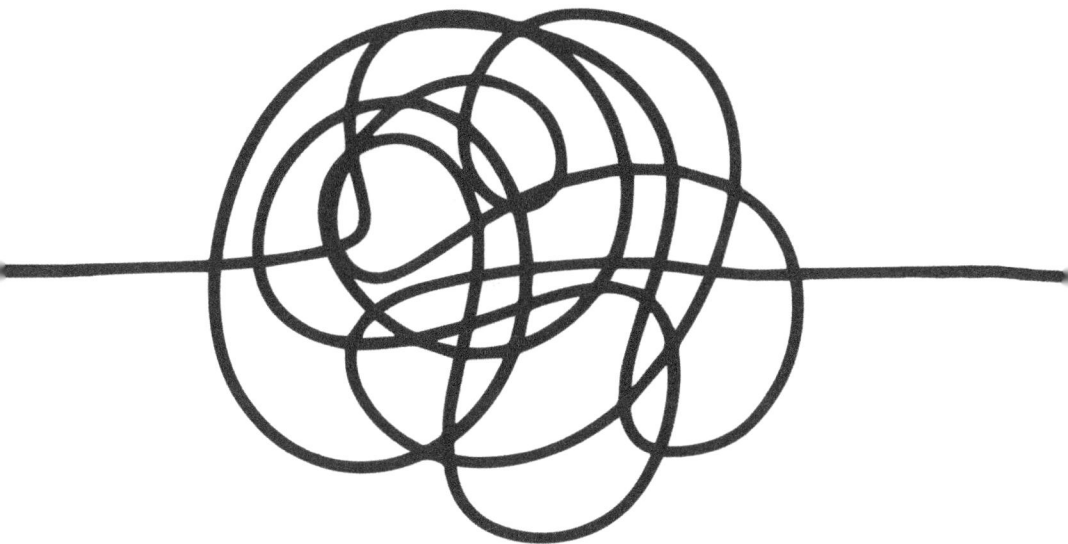

ENGAGING COMPLEXITY:
OPERATIONAL SHIFTS

The purpose of shifting your mindsets, as described in part II, becomes evident here in part III. New thinking about marketing in a VUCA world opens the door to new actions—and it's the actions that produce more advantageous marketing outcomes. As your mind shifts, you will likely see many opportunities to do things differently. And to start you down this path, in part III, I focus on four capabilities where a ComplexityWise approach will make a big difference in determining success. Each chapter explains several operational shifts pertaining to that area.

- **The Information System: Collective Intelligence:** The development and connection of the organization's brains—human and machine—improves a sense of what is happening in the system and, where possible, anticipates what's ahead. Intelligence practices include thinking skills, the use of various kinds of technology (e.g., data, analytics, artificial intelligence) and associated approaches, information sources, and methods for human-machine collaboration. Collective intelligence is explored in chapter 7.

- **The Organization: Integrated Teams:** The people piece of ComplexityWise marketing requires integrating the organization into multidisciplinary squads that are coordinated, guided, supplied with resources, and linked with organizational bridges and shared infrastructure. These teams can start in marketing and expand to include more functions at the company's edge. Many of the skills that are today isolated in the marketing silo are needed all across the company, and expanding integration into an organizational network adds further value. Integrated teams is explored in chapter 8.

- **The Work Method: An Agile Operation:** Effective response in a VUCA environment depends on an organization's ability to gather feedback about what is happening, adapt strategies and tactics to the situation, and then act. All of this must be done quickly and accurately. An agile operation within the context of ComplexityWise marketing takes advantage of more formal Agile (spelled with a capital A) marketing practices and which work better in VUCA settings than traditional operations. How this applies to marketing is explored in chapter 9.

- **The Change Management Method: Leveraging Emergence:** Systems constantly change and although you can't control them, you can steer. This chapter adds to the marketing leader's tool kit some approaches to transformation that leverage the powerful process of emergence characteristics of complex systems. Change and emergence are explored in chapter 10.

Within each capability chapter are contained conditioning practices which improve market system health by making the VUCA environment more conducive to beneficial outcomes. Other practices strengthen marketing's agility. They emphasize awareness, speed, flexibility, creativity, problem-solving, and the ability to take optimal action.

Developing ComplexityWise capabilities is like mastering a sport. Each beneficial practice improves others, like consistent strength training improves the time it takes to recover from injury. There is no point at which you are "done" developing. Results begin to appear after a moderate stretch of practice and improve with continuous effort. Defining an end point that is "good enough" depends on what you want to achieve. A nine-year-old with three years of practice and instruction can be good enough to play Little League. A New York Yankee's player needs a lot more skill and experience. Consider these operational shifts to be the beginning of an ever-growing playbook as leaders in marketing and other professions learn more about how to succeed in our turbulent world.

CHAPTER 7

THE INFORMATION SYSTEM: COLLECTIVE INTELLIGENCE

*Explanations exist; they have existed for all time;
there is always a well-known solution to every human problem—
neat, plausible, and wrong.*

—**H.L. Mencken,** *Prejudices: Second Series*

I sat in a sales meeting listening to sales managers prepare their quarterly revenue forecast for management. My mission was to help salespeople close faster, and I needed firsthand information about their situation. As the managers combed through reports from the CRM (customer relationship management) system account by account, rep by rep, they commented on their findings.

"There's no way that Company A deal is going to come through this quarter," said one. "Reduce that probability to 20 percent." "Company B projection seems low," mused another. "Chris is sandbagging." As the meeting progressed, I learned that Matt rarely enters deals into the system until right before they close so managers won't hound him for updates, while Lauren's strong customer relationships enabled her to bring deals in quickly.

Throughout the morning, the group adjusted here and tweaked there until they collectively agreed on what they called a "judged" number. It bore little resemblance to the forecast presented by the CRM system. Having worked with salespeople for years (and married to one), nothing I learned at that meeting surprised me. Much to the confusion of my boss, the general manager, the judged number was usually within 5 percent of quarter-end revenue. He was happy, of course, but frustrated that the sales managers couldn't explain exactly how they arrived at their number.

The more accurate refereed forecast was made possible by collective intelligence. The CRM system provided important data points, but the secret sauce was cooked by pooling private information each manager alone possessed. Collective intelligence was smarter and more accurate than any single source. Information is so essential for marketing to thrive in a VUCA world that success is impossible without it. This is why I've selected shifting information operations in the direction of collective intelligence as the first of the capabilities discussed in this section.

In this chapter, I explore how to develop marketing processes where collective intelligence is the norm, integrating human and technical capabilities including artificial intelligence. It is not a blueprint for specific information technology systems. These continually advance and must be designed to meet the specific needs to each business. Instead, I've identified attributes for marketing's information processes that will be most useful for improving agility and market system health.

THE HUMAN-TECHNOLOGY COLLABORATION

Collective intelligence means connecting the organization's brains—human and technological—to develop and maintain the greatest possible sense of what is happening, to anticipate change where possible, and provide insight for navigation and decisions. Companies must work toward an organizational neural network, fusing operations with this kind of a hybrid intelligence system. Collective intelligence is where agility starts. It feeds the mindset of a successful navigator who needs situational awareness to decide on the next best action, informs investors, guides statisticians, and advises ecologists. Customer-facing employees need intelligence about customer context. The better your sense of what's going on, the more accurate your response will be. To accomplish this task, technology systems and people each bring to the table complementary intelligence skills.

Technology as an Intelligence Collaborator

ComplexityWise marketing would be impossible without intelligence technology. Edward Lorenz would never have discovered the non-linearity of weather without his Royal McBee LGP-30 computer,[1] and just like our brains are insufficient to figure out the weather, humans are unequipped to sort through the mountains of data required to find the patterns inherent in complex markets. To see what is unseeable with the naked eye, we need technology. Microscopes, MRIs, telescopes, and thermal imaging help us see the hidden physical world, and it takes information technology to observe the trends we can't see in systems.

Marketing technology (martech) is a broad field. The 2024 Martech industry landscape[2] published by chiefmartec.com offers over 14,000 possibilities for applications, a 41.8 percent compound annual growth rate (CAGR) from thirteen years earlier. The six major categories are Advertising & Promotion, Content & Experience, Social & Relationships, Commerce & Sales, Data, and Management. A company's martech "stack" typically contains dozens, sometimes hundreds of applications, although, arguably, many are underutilized.

The most obvious use of martech is to deliver digital marketing capability and improve marketing productivity. However, the tools also offer two benefits related to complexity and unpredictability. One, they help to wrestle a greater variety, volume, and velocity of activities in the following ways:

- Serves as guide rails in fast-moving situations to direct action and steer marketers away from hazards in the way that guide rails on a mountain bobsled run aligns the crew with the path where the fastest time is expected

- Reduces lag time and removes distance, allowing geographically dispersed teams to work together

- Encodes and preserves the data, content, conversations, and processes that form marketing's memory

- Controls some of the massive number of "stupid but critical" elements that can explode in complex environments, such as when a rebranding initiative requires replacing hundreds of old logos from self-evident items, such as the website, to those easily overlooked, such as invoices

And two, these systems, along with those in other company areas, produce the data needed for collective intelligence. An abundance of trusted data along with appropriate analysis gives marketers the best chance of finding the signals, especially the highly important early signals that correlate to revenue and other outcomes. Data informs and inspires creativity and finds interesting patterns that aid strategy and problem-solving. Bill Schmarzo, the "Dean of Big Data" and author of several popular books on the topic, says it well: "In this digitally-transforming world, the only source of sustainable and defensible competitive differentiation is the organization's ability to exploit the economic value of its data and analytic assets to deliver analytics-infused customer, product, service, and operational outcomes."[3]

Artificial Intelligence (AI) in Marketing

Many martech tools already utilize artificial intelligence (AI), and the field is progressing amazingly fast. It is difficult to predict the ways AI will impact future marketing. One thing we know for sure is that AI will render aspects of marketing jobs archaic, as innovation always has, while generating new and interesting opportunities.

AI works by *consuming* data about past decisions, for example what words earlier writers chose to place next in a sentence or what content earlier customers decided to view. It then *analyzes* this data to discern patterns and trends, and uses algorithms to *predict* what element (i.e., word, content, picture, action, media placement) is most likely to happen next, thus increasing the probability of a desired outcome (i.e., meaningful sentence, engagement, conversion, purchase, efficiency). Today, three significant uses of the technology include predictive AI (which analyzes data to provide forecasts, recommendations, and insights), generative AI (which produces new outputs from earlier created datasets such as texts, images, and code), and AI agents (which layer decision-making and action capability onto underlying analytical capability to perform tasks). AI adapts and learns as it goes. Uses of AI in marketing include chatbots, personalized email campaigns, writing content, ad purchasing and placement, and several kinds of analysis. Some AIs use Natural Language Processing (NLP) technology, which enables the AI to understand human-type communication, so you don't have to be a data scientist to leverage AI's power.

AI can tirelessly perform repetitious decision tasks that tend to irritate humans, such as customizing emails, dynamically optimizing content, and ad bidding. Any designer who has gone home with bleeding eyeballs from painstakingly removing background from a photograph will attest to this advantage. But it's not just low-end work that AI helps. AI can also guide marketing work, accelerating some tasks and improving the quality of others. Decisions requiring memory or judgment such as communicating, problem-solving, and advising are aided by AI's ability to remind people of what worked (or didn't) in the past. Recommendation engines are one example of this guidance capability.

Since the efficacy of AI depends on the data it has been trained on, most

AIs perform best on narrow, focused tasks where a large amount of excellent data is available. Marketing's VUCA world is anything but narrow and focused, and because of this complexity there are risks to applying AI in a marketing setting without plenty of supervision. Nicholas Bostrum, in the book *Superintelligence: Paths, Dangers, and Strategies*[4] offers an example of a machine simulation that, when given the task of ferrying a passenger to the airport as quickly as possible, has no reservations about running over pedestrians.

Despite its increasing intelligence, AI typically fails when interpreting ambiguity and nuance. While this capability may improve in the future, today AI is very literal. For example, the 2014 movie *Her* features Scarlett Johansson as a brilliant virtual assistant. In real life, the AI algorithms flop when generalizing tasks into broader contexts than they were trained for.

Causal AI

"There are no simple solutions to complex problems," state the authors of *Causal Artificial Intelligence: The Next Step in Effective Business AI.*[5] Although the causes of marketing outcomes will always be couched in probabilities, causal inference is the scientific method that helps identify them. The method is broadly used across science but is very difficult and is especially challenging in situations where experiments cannot be conducted. Causal AI is an emerging field that uses algorithms to run through difficult statistical analysis.

In the causal inference method, a team of knowledgeable people including data scientists, subject matter experts, data experts, technologists, business managers, and executives collectively identify the most likely sources of data and the best questions to ask. Causal AI can then assist with the heavy lifting. Without human guidance, AI can send businesses in some strange directions.

Human Intelligence as an Intelligence Collaborator

Having evolved in nature's complex arena, humans are well suited for performing in ambiguous and nuanced situations. We excel at creativity, critical thinking, judgment, problem-solving, and interpersonal skills. We grasp context and we can improvise in the face of new situations. For example, we can sense meaning in a customer's inflection change and evaluate the subtle trade-offs such as giving a money-losing discount today to increase future loyalty. Humans also excel at physically dexterous work beyond the scope of technology's capability.

The combination of AI-infused automation with human competencies has the potential to improve the market system. As AI reduces some marketing tasks, it makes time for human collaborators to focus on the attributes they best contribute to collective intelligence. The most relevant competencies that *humans* will provide include the following:

- Critical thinking (e.g., conceptualizing, questioning, decision monitoring and correction, applying scientific and design methods)

- Problem-solving (e.g., identifying, analysis, prioritization, alternative selection)

- Governance, including governance of AI (e.g., security, ethics, privacy, consent, bias control)

- Innovation and creativity (e.g., social, experiences, content)

- Interpersonal skills (e.g., listening, empathy, communication, negotiation, persuasion)

- Behavioral sciences (e.g., psychology, economics, organizational)

- Bespoke production (e.g., making, expediting, constructing)

FOUR PRACTICES TO GENERATE COLLECTIVE INTELLIGENCE

The following four areas offer advantageous operational shifts to improve marketing effectiveness in a VUCA world.

1. Improve data management

2. Support radical transparency around information

3. Upskill your use of analytics

4. Help humans and machines collaborate

Undoubtably, market leaders will have already begun to implement some of these. If so, the guidance is to prioritize and accelerate. And, of course, start down the path of any shifts that are new. Let's explore these four areas.

Practice 1: Improve Data Management

Useful intelligence depends on quality data, but most companies lack this indispensable ingredient. As one CMO wisecracked, "'We have the best customer data!' said no one ever." There are many sources for information on how to appropriately manage data, and companies often do a good job of managing their internal data from financial and operational systems. But data from the edge functions (e.g., marketing, sales, customer service) blends external and internal interactions and is subject to high change, making data management more challenging. For ComplexityWise marketing, pay special attention to these factors:

- **Data diversity:** Insight improves with data from multiple sources across the market value chain (e.g., marketing, sales, finance, media, partners). Shift attention from data gathered from primarily internal and centralized sources to include data that comes from the outside and data reflecting interactions at the company edge. Complement data systems with deep information from in-person experiences, stories, and rich media like video.

- **Data quality:** Quality in, quality out. Many companies suffer from poorly documented sales cycles, bad firmographics, incomplete buyer analysis, and failure to collect adequate budget data. Despite the recommendation to increase data diversity, a small amount of good quality data is better than lots of junk. Technologies such as data cleansing and harmonizing services can help overcome some data quality problems. Look out for significant alterations in market context that may strongly disrupt data patterns. After a period of big change, such as the COVID pandemic, the validity of older data may need to be questioned.

- **Data time signatures:** Time remains a thorny issue for the constantly changing market. Due to the lag time for effects to appear in complex systems, shift from looking only at near-term data to include data with multiple time signatures (e.g., historical, real-time, leading) in your analysis. Apply each type as needed to answer the appropriate questions. Only with a longer view will you begin to appreciate changes in market system health. Highly dynamic situations will benefit from more frequent data updates, so shortening intervals between measurements also helps.

Practice 2: Support Radical Transparency Around Information

It's one thing to have quality intelligence; it's another to get that intelligence to the people who need it when they need it. For greatest agility, teams need as complete a picture as possible. Companies must shift from "need to know" to a collaborative culture where insights and results are shared broadly within the company, not just inside teams or with departmental managers.

One of the best examples of the value of intelligence transparency can be found in General Stanley McChrystal's book, *Team of Teams*.[6] In it, McChrystal describes how, when he got to Iraq, he found the coalition forces failing despite their astounding force and exceptional planning. Al Qaeda was fluid, and before the coalition could plan and decide on a course of action against the group, the situation had changed. As often happens, the generals before McChrystal had doubled down on what had worked in the past. Their top-down plans got more detailed and more controlled. They provided even better machines. It didn't work. One of the first and most effective actions McChrystal instituted was to break down the information silos that had formed between the different experts and institute what he called radical transparency. He built a system that ensured that operators at the edge and the intelligence agents back at HQ had full access to what the other knew. The traditional hierarchical approach to information had to go. Centralization had to go.

In traditional organizations, intelligence doesn't easily flow. Clogs form accidently when people forget to share beyond their group, are unaware of the need to share, or lack the facility to do so. Other blocks form intentionally. Information is power, and in a competitive culture, having it can make people feel strong. People in tight silos or in hierarchical echelons tend to hoard data. For example, marketers may withhold useful research data from content experiments from sales, for example, because it is viewed as sensitive or strategic. While some information is indeed risky to share, often the consequences of blocking are even worse and are silent killers of effectiveness and productivity.

Siloed data breeds unnecessary mistrust and results in poorer decisions based on insufficient information. Customers bounce around, and outcomes are influenced by many parts of the company. Any customer data could provide important insights, not just data about what marketing has done. For example, one company found that tracking customer engagement from service documents on their website was a strong indicator of product interest.

A culture of transparency removes barriers to productivity and reduces bureaucratic impediments. Some practices companies can undertake to increase transparency include:

- **Conduct open discussions:** Rather than routinely handing down objectives, strategies, and accountability metrics, inform these with frequent formal and informal feedback. Explore results collectively, sharing them with other teams as well as with leaders and sometimes with stakeholders (including customers) or their representatives. Shift exchanges from primarily top-down to primarily lateral (many-to-many) and bottom-up. Welcome more external feedback.

- **Expose more work elements:** Make marketing's work more visible. Discuss schedules, priorities, decision context, progress, and methods in a relatively unfiltered way, as it helps others understand how they fit it and can help.

- **Reduce unnecessary variation:** Marketing, like any other function, has necessary specialization, but much jargon and unique practices make intelligence transmission more difficult. I once facilitated the resolution of a contentious argument between two groups who were warring over direction. It took weeks to cut through a mountain of special terms, group-specific data, and competing frameworks only to find that the real disagreement was over one item. While it wasn't an inconsequential decision, the teams (with some management intervention) were able to make an informed choice and move forward.

- **Make the workplace psychologically safe:** W. Edwards Deming wrote, "Fear invites wrong figures."[7] People must feel comfortable sharing information and feedback, even when negative. Amy Edmondson, Harvard Business School professor and author of *The Fearless Organization*,[8] says that psychological safety is an emergent group phenomenon, which means that appropriate management practices create fertile ground for this team attribute to develop. Practices include setting clear expectations, encouraging listening, and showing humility and appreciation when people speak up.

Practice 3: Upskill Your Use of Analytics

Upskilling, in this context, means reducing reliance on cheap and easy analytic styles (which don't work) and investing in more advanced styles, which are often more expensive and difficult (but which work much better). The cheap and easy analytics are common rules-based styles, such as attribution, which rely on a priori assumptions. The more advanced and appropriate styles are methods used in probability-affected sciences, which can discover the trends and causes in tangled systems. A comparison of two situations—one stable and one dynamic—helps illustrate what is needed.

The Old Faithful geyser in Yellowstone National Park is a well-known tourist attraction. Park visitors can easily predict its eruption if they understand the famous clockwork rule that gives the geyser its name. Every 45–125 minutes, the geyser faithfully performs. Eruptions of the park's Beehive Geyser, on the other hand, are less predictable. Its eruptions are erratic, occurring every few hours to a few days. Yet park rangers can reliably steer eager tourists to see the spectacular natural show. How do they do it? The rangers have help with predicting the Beehive's eruptions. A tiny white mini-geyser reliably puffs from the ground nearby exactly fifteen to twenty minutes before the Beehive erupts. This mini-geyser is called an indicator geyser, and it serves as a weak signal that predicts the big event. When rangers see the indicator geyser blow, they can quickly gather park visitors to view the spectacular big brother.

Market systems are a bit like the Beehive, non-linear but semipredictable if you can find some sort of indictor. Hints about the future abound, if only we can find them, and this requires the appropriate type of analytics.

The Limitations of Rules-Based Attribution

Rules-based attribution is possibly the most common and the most misleading type of analytics used in marketing. Attribution is the ROI method that apportions revenue (or other financial outcomes such as pipeline value) to identifiable marketing tactics. Companies are attracted to attribution because it seems to offer a fast, simple method for matching outcomes to costs. On the positive side, attribution applications provide valuable insights into the steps individual customers tend to take toward purchase, but when applied to ROI, attribution offers a false narrative.

Figure 7.1: Marketing attribution is a whimsy.

Marketers know this—or at least suspect it. A coffee mug from Thot Leader Labs, an ecommerce store offering gifts and apparel inspired by tech industry humor, with the slogan "Marketing attribution is fake . . . we literally made it up" (figure 7.1) received an explosion of laughter emojis and exclamations of "I need this!" from the marketing community on social media. What marketers "make up" are predefined rules (e.g., first touch, last touch, multitouch, time decay) that attempt to match a specific tactic to revenue.

Attribution obscures marketing's interdependences. When you purchase a car, how can you attribute portions of the price you paid to the billboard you saw last month, the recommendation from your brother-in-law at a party two weeks ago, the TV ad last week, the ad on Instagram the day before, and the location of the dealership? Marketing cannot be reduced to the sum of its parts.

Attribution also hinders marketers from finding the real contributors to revenue uplift because simplistic conclusions can lead to faulty decisions.

A client told me about how a CFO insisted that the majority of marketing budget be spent on product demos because demos clearly had the best ROI based on "last touch" analysis. This mandate alarmed the heads of sales and marketing, who knew that removing other marketing programs would lead to revenue declines within months.

The Value of Statistical Analysis

The appropriate kind of marketing analytics uses the data we *do* know in order to discover things we *don't* know. Multivariate regression analysis is a statistical methodology that helps us explore potential causal relationships between many factors simultaneously. It is a common analytics technique used in marketing and underlies most investigations in science and economics.

While employing the supercomputer powers required for weather prediction isn't necessary for multivariate regression analysis, the approach is essentially the same. Data scientists look for relationships between a single dependent metric (for ROI this would be the financial "R" marker) and two or more independent variables (for marketing this would be a range of possible contributing tactics). Using this method, analysts can find the best "fit" correlating today's revenue with past interactions.

Multivariate regression analysis helps marketers answer questions such as "What is the probability of outcome X?" "Can we find the biggest contributors (or inhibitors) to outcome X?" and "What are early indicators that outcome X is likely to happen?" This last question is key. If we can learn about a probable outcome earlier, we give ourselves more time to prepare for a response or to take action to intervene. Although finding exact predictable causes for outcomes is impossible, some marketing tactics *do* matter more than others. Answering the question "Can we safely eliminate any tactics?" allows marketers to reduce or reallocate budget. Marketers also want to understand "What are optimal tactics and sequences?" to tease out, for example, the 20 percent of known programs that best correlate with business outcomes. To illustrate, analytics may find that a rise in social sentiment nine months ago correlates with closed deals this quarter. Initiating a new pay-per-click (PPC) campaign may correlate with higher web sales.

Because multivariate regression analysis, which is used in marketing mix modeling (MMM), examines multiple factors simultaneously, we can explore the interdependency of the many factors. Each factor analyzed is scored, and those with the highest score will be those with the greatest (but not necessarily the only) contribution. MMM also provides information about the probability of success, just as a weather app will tell you there is a 50 percent chance of rain on Tuesday. A good model will inform marketers about the volatility in a particular element of the marketing mix. Still, decision-makers must remember that this type of modeling will never deliver vending machine–type certainty.

Despite its promise, MMM has drawbacks:

- MMM remains relatively expensive, although automation is decreasing its cost and required effort.

- MMM can be time-consuming. Finding the best "fit" requires repetition, especially when there are many factors to consider in the algorithm. Machine-learning technology is helping to speed this repetition.

- MMM can only draw conclusions based on available data. When data sources are limited or poor, models may undervalue or miss important correlations.

- MMM measures only what you have already implemented. It's possible that a strategy you haven't tried could perform better. Exploring and testing new possibilities is an important part of any marketing strategy.

Practice 4: Help Humans and Machines Collaborate

As the technology collaborator in collective intelligence becomes more capable, human partners can abandon some tasks and must take up others. Some of these skills will be technical, but martech continues to get easier to use, and deep data management is best assigned to experts. Abilities that move to the forefront include those that are uniquely human, as described in the section on human intelligence collaborators, and those that marketers must master to get the best from technology.

One operational shift suggests accelerating the migration of marketing processes to a hybrid model that "blends human and machine intelligence in a redesigned business process to achieve better outcomes than either humans or machines could achieve alone," say the authors of *Augmented Intelligence*.[9] Redesign will be iterative, improving as the organization learns. When technologies first get invented, people use them to make the *current* way of doing things better-faster-cheaper. It's not until we get some facility and comfort with new tech that business process innovation emerges. A fresh look at the customer journey reveals opportunities for this kind of hybridization.

Take, for example, the mid-funnel phase of the journey where customers evaluate alternatives. Marketers and salespeople are aware that customers bounce between digital and human interactions, making the traditional, linear, first-marketing-then-sales process archaic. Instead, customers enjoy digital, self-directed education, and this task can be aided by AI-curated content, AI-enabled prototyping, dynamic pricing, and emotional-AI enhanced chat. But when customers get stuck—and this could happen at any time—they want a human problem-solver to investigate, discern emotions, match unique situations to appropriate solutions, and persuade and build consensus. As one buyer told me, "It's like Home Depot. I want to look on my own until I have a question, then I need that guy in the orange apron, and he better know what he is talking about."

Another recommended shift toward human-machine collaboration is to ensure marketers train in the new skills needed for working with AI. Partnering well with AI requires many new capabilities, including training, managing, troubleshooting, decision-making, governance, and ethics. The authors of a *Harvard Business Review* article, "Why You Aren't Getting More from Your Marketing AI,"[10] describe how a consumer products firm reduced the error rate in their sales-volume forecast from 25 percent to 17 percent, yet lost money despite improved accuracy. While human decision-makers could tell that the underlying intent of error reduction was improving profits, the AI was ignorant of this assumption. The AI had improved precision in the low-margin products where most errors had been produced but had inadvertently reduced accuracy in high-margin products. This unintended consequence caused the company to underestimate demand for their most profitable products.

One of the most important human skills needing improvement is the art of questioning. Eugene Ionesco, Romanian French playwright said, "It is not the answer that enlightens, but the question."[11] The efficacy of AI relies on effective *prompt engineering*[12] because inferior questions, inaccurate or poorly articulated, lead to useless answers, some of which could be substantially damaging. Marketers must learn how to work with data scientists to get the most useful answers from AI.

Mastering the art of questioning will also help marketers in other information-oriented ways. ComplexityWise marketing needs critical thinkers: people with strong skills to conceptualize, synthesize, evaluate, and make judgments. Critical thinkers aren't necessarily looking for "*the* answer" but rather a path to learn and grow. Kids, with their chains of follow-up questions, are delightful models. "How does a zipper work?" "Why did they do it that way?" "What would happen if I did this instead?" To ask good questions, we must understand the nature of what we don't know. We must avoid grasping at answers simply to shut down the uneasy feeling that comes with uncertainty.

TAKE THIS AWAY

Intelligence is one of the foundational capabilities needed to thrive in VUCA markets. Advancements in information technology have provided and continue to provide crucial insights into the way systems work. The human brains of marketing offer complementary qualities. The recommended shift is from an operation that separates various intelligence elements—whether accidently or on purpose—toward a fusion into a hybrid collective intelligence that integrates what technology, including AI, and humans do best. Collective intelligence offers the optimal path toward thriving in a VUCA world.

To upscale your information systems, do the following:

- **Improve data management.** The bedrock of useful intelligence is data, and there is probably no way a business today can overachieve in data management. Data diversity, quality, and the availability of data with multiple time signatures is key.

- **Support radical transparency around information.** To see the most accurate path forward, marketers need as complete a picture as possible. Remove impediments from the flow of important intelligence.

- **Upskill your use of analytics.** Simplistic analytics won't work for complex environments like markets. Techniques suited for marketing, especially multivariate regression analysis, respect the multi-causal VUCA nature and deliver more useful answers.

- **Help humans and machines collaborate.** As technology advances, the role of human participants evolves. Successful organizations will develop hybrid marketing processes combining the best of both worlds and develop new skills to get the most out of new intelligence tools.

CHAPTER 8

THE ORGANIZATION: INTEGRATED TEAMS

Talent wins games, but teamwork and intelligence win championships.

—**Michael Jordan,** *American athlete*

A few years ago, I had eye surgery. It wasn't major surgery, so I was awake through the procedure, and it was fascinating to watch the medical team at work—from prepping me at my arrival, through the surgery, to sending me safely home. It occurred to me that an operating room team is the quintessential effective, customer-centered team.

A surgical team consists of different specialists, and although each expert has a unique job and different skills, they collaborate. Each specialist knows their role and coordinates accordingly. The team shares a common mission, which is the patient's health and safety; they are empowered to make decisions about patient care and are accountable for those decisions. Behind the scenes is a support system ensuring the care team has full transparency into the patient's context along with the tools, training, and technology needed to do their job. Fortunately, my surgery was routine. But if something unexpected had happened, I trusted the surgical team was agile enough to respond appropriately.

The surgical team illustrates what leaders in many turbulent environments have learned: that effectiveness in a complex environment relies on the initiative of people at the enterprise "edge" who have local situational knowledge as well as the capability to take optimal action. Success at the edge where the enterprise meets its customers must become everyone's most important objective, just like great health systems prioritize their patient care teams and sports franchises fixate on field or court success.

Achieving this degree of agility and fostering the customer centricity that supports not only today's revenue but also builds market system health requires a way of organizing different from the traditional hierarchy of departmental silos. What is needed is integrated teams—multidisciplinary and abundantly connected.

In this chapter, I discuss the benefits of team integration and share how integration can be achieved at three levels, starting with integrating at the marketing level and then progressively harmonizing marketing with more company functions. Also included in this chapter are six practices to effectively manage integrated teams.

BRING THE ORGANIZATION TOGETHER

There are many kinds of groups. Some are teams; some are not. Just gathering people together and calling them a team isn't accomplishing anything significant. A team that makes a difference in a complex environment must share the right combination of attributes and be managed in the right way. For this chapter I use the term *squad* to differentiate a special type of team that works optimally for VUCA markets. Some companies that have created squads have used the terms pods, cells, or other special names to describe them. The exact name isn't important. However, how squads are organized and managed matters a lot.

A squad is multidisciplinary and highly connected in ways that are less hierarchical than conventional organizations. Usually, each squad is small, consisting of six to ten people with varying skill sets. Their work orients around the delivery of some aspect of customer value rather than internally defined functions. They are encouraged to be self-managing. During the COVID crisis, McKinsey & Company advised clients needing a speedy response to develop such structures in key areas of the company, describing them as "a cohesive and adaptable network of teams, united by a common purpose, that gathers information, devises solutions, puts them into practice, refines outcomes—and does it all *fast*."[1] McKinsey noted how companies that took this path for emergency purposes were so happy with the results that they began exploring ways to make it permanent.

Squads and networks of squads enhance organizational capability in the following ways:

- **Increased speed and productivity:** Information flow, decision-making, acting, and getting feedback happen faster with fewer layers and greater connection. When people with all the core skills necessary to solve the problem are connected in a collaborative, well-oiled squad, they can avoid the delay of seeking or negotiating the skills, information, or approvals needed to act.

- **Broader and deeper intelligence:** Critical knowledge becomes exposed that previously became lost or hidden between hand-offs and layers. Information sharing is enhanced, and integration removes incentives for people to withhold information or game the system. Diversity of views, ways of thinking, even life experiences contribute to greater insights, problem-solving capability, error correcting, and bias avoidance.

- **Improved coordination and adaptability:** People better understand their role in the big picture. Common missions and multiple links reduce the tendency to foster local objectives that are often in conflict. In silos, problems always seem to arise elsewhere, making solutions more difficult.

- **Better customer experience:** Employees no longer sequestered in specialist silos can more easily see missing or faulty steps in processes, so the customer experience feels more seamless and smoother.

- **Greater innovation:** Exposure to new ideas and challenges boosts opportunities for creative and cross-functional solutions. "Group think" and "collective stupidity" can be reduced.

- **Improved employee morale:** Employees with an expanded sphere of influence are motivated to help solve problems. Employees feel like they are a part of something greater.

To gain these benefits, marketing needs to move beyond its conventional silos and into these multidisciplinary, highly connected squads. In most organizations, silos form almost without thought, fostered for so long by Taylor's scientific management approach. Professionals who do different work, such as finance and marketing, are segregated into departments. Even within marketing, people are grouped by functional specialty or channel (e.g., advertising, events, digital, field). The impetus to form silos is so strong that often when I've talked to marketing leaders who are organizing initiatives requiring a range of expertise, I have found that their first impulse is to create yet one more silo. There are some advantages to silos. It's easy and efficient to hire, train, and manage people whose work is relatively homogeneous. Yet, when it comes to working in complex environments, the drawbacks overshadow the benefits.

Before diving deeper into the ways marketing can be integrated, I lay the groundwork by further describing what squads and multi-linked networks of squads look like and how these structures differ from a conventional organization.

Multidisciplinary Teams (Squads) vs. Silos

Figure 8.1 compares an integrated multidisciplinary configuration with traditional departments organized by expertise. Integration brings together *in one squad* the primary skills needed to provide something that a customer finds valuable, such as buying support, information, or service. Note in the illustration how many of the people in the integrated version are members of more than one team. Like a matrix, they are on a squad as well as another team. Their primary squad association is mission based, shown as the vertical orientation, and dotted lines show the team members' association with other complementary teams, such as expertise guilds. More about mission orientation and various links is discussed further in this chapter.

In contrast, in traditional organizations where people are housed in silos, links with other groups (if they exist at all) are either informal, governed by elaborate alignment SLAs (service level agreements), or managed via executive relationships.

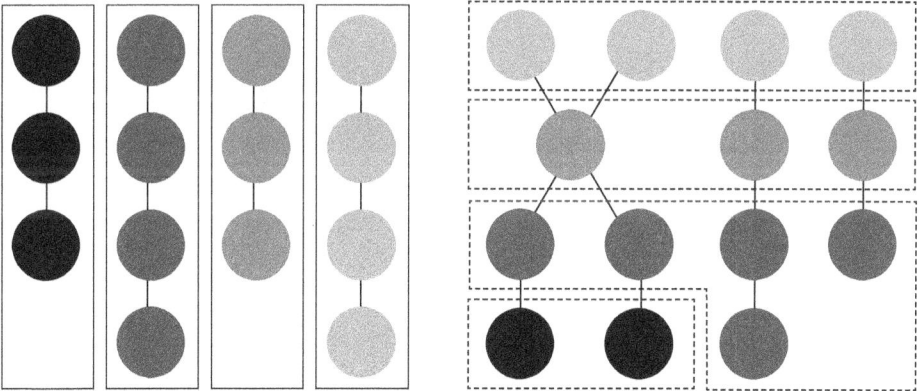

Figure 8.1: Comparing Traditional Silo Structure with Multidisciplinary Teams

In a traditional, siloed organization (left), people who do similar or related work are organized into vertical groups. In contrast, when companies organize around multidisciplinary teams, people with different functions work together in different combinations.

Multi-Linked Networks vs. Hierarchies

In a more fully integrated organization, squads will be part of a highly linked organizational network. Figure 8.2 contrasts conventional hierarchies with multiple layers, with managers "above" having more power and authority than those "below" with a network that has fewer layers. Networks can be formed in a variety of configurations. The illustration, which shows several linked squads with other company teams, looks a little messy when compared to the neat and clean boxes of a hierarchy, but this web is powerfully purposeful. In a hierarchy, information flows are primarily vertical with few lateral connections. In a network, information, ideas, and expertise flows quickly to where it is needed. Some hierarchy is retained for legal purposes and structural coordination. More about these network elements is described later in the chapter.

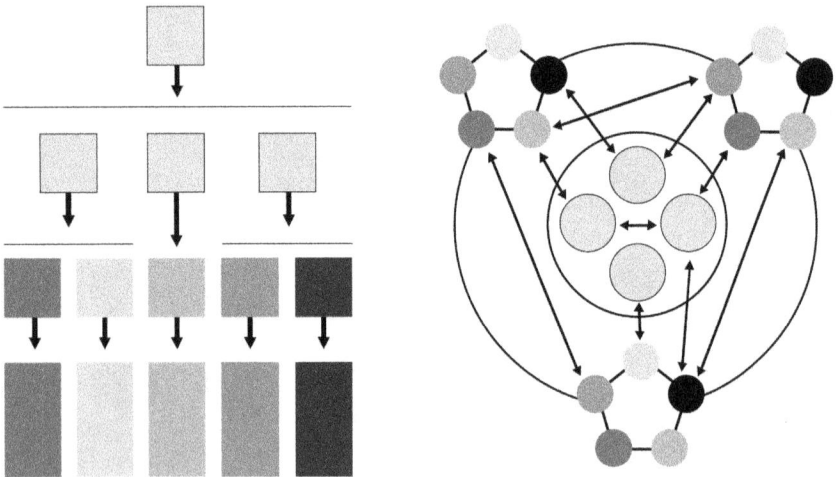

Figure 8.2: Hierarchies vs. Networks

In a traditional, siloed organization, power and decision-making are very much top-down.
In contrast, each node in a networked organization has some authority to act on its own,
coordinated by top leaders.

Three Levels of Integration

Marketing plays a significant role in integrated organizations, and marketing leaders can gain advantages right away by integrating their current teams. Eventually, companies may want to extend the value by incorporating more teams beyond marketing.

Level 1—Connecting Marketing: The first level of a squad can be created within the CMO's span of control by integrating marketers with different skills. Companies have created squads for use in account-based marketing/account-based GTM (go-to-market), Agile Marketing, or digital marketing, as well as for special projects.

The CMO of a large tech services company used a project-based marketing squad, which he called a tiger team, to quickly scale his account-based marketing program. Squads formed around role-based personas (such as the chief data officer). Each squad had eight members: a leader plus seven specialists (analytics, content, web/inbound, outbound, communications, sales enablement, and social). Everyone was measured on the same goal—closed deals within the identified account list. In four months, the CMO met his goal of scaling to nearly one hundred ABM programs. The sales team was ecstatic. One sales manager suggested that the company "fire ten salespeople and put the money into marketing."

Level 2—Connecting the Company Edge: Further integration connects marketing with other edge functions such as sales, product experts, and service people and puts them into squads that I call *customer value squads* because each squad is oriented around delivering some aspect of a customer-centric mission, ranging from product or service development and extending through the entire customer relationship. Depending on the mission, some squads may consist only of people currently in marketing, but most will be a mix of current departments. Every squad will likely need some marketing expertise. Analytics, content development, and digital media expertise will be most needed.

The Canadian software company SMART Technologies recognized that the growing misalignment between how they were selling and how customers were buying resulted in missed opportunities and, due to traditional silos, costly duplication in messaging, analytics, and technology. Their solution was to dismantle their sales, marketing, and service silos and reconfigure the approximately two hundred fifty employees into multidisciplinary, geographically aligned "Unified Commercial Engines (UCE) PODS." The UCE PODS are mapped to five customer-centric "jobs to be done" (value tasks) oriented around the modern digital-forward customer-centric purchase and use journey. These tasks were learn, buy, order/install, adopt, and support. The UCEs were supported by three centers of excellence focused on data and analytics, customer insights and positioning, and creative and digital experience. In the first eighteen months of the new organization, despite being further complicated by the pandemic, lead volume increased 50 percent, lead acceptance 35 percent, and year-over-year revenue growth by 48 percent.[2]

Level 3—Connecting the company: Squads can be further integrated into a company-wide network of squads connected to other teams that collectively encompasses all or most of its functions. Moving to a network at the company level is a C-suite and possibly board of directors–level decision. CMOs can't get to this level of integration on their own, but since some progressive companies are moving in this direction and networks offer the greatest possibility of agility and additional business value, I would be remiss if I didn't share with marketing leaders where this movement is going.

One example of a networked company is the pioneering health services company Buurtzorg, headquartered in the Netherlands. Situating nurses in Dutch neighborhoods has been a common practice since the nineteenth century. Throughout the twentieth century, these groups absorbed industrial-era methods such as organizing by skill specialization and hierarchical control. In 2006, Buurtzorg[3] was founded with a radically different approach—self-management. Buurtzorg's "onion" model centers around self-managing clients (patients) supported by a self-managed neighborhood team of twelve nurses.

Each team collectively organizes, shares work, and makes decisions on everything from administration and finance to customizing and delivering healthcare. As Buurtzorg scaled to eight hundred fifty nurse-led community teams, the corporate group has stayed small, providing coaching, training, and support rather than what would typically be called management. The company has achieved outrageously positive results. It is more efficient. According to the company website and a number of reputable publications, a 2009 Ernst & Young study estimated that the Dutch system would save 40 percent of costs if all healthcare were delivered in this model of care.[4] In other studies, client (patient) satisfaction was 30 percent higher than average, and improved employee satisfaction was measured by lower absenteeism and turnover.[5]

SIX PRACTICES TO FOSTER HIGH-PERFORMING INTEGRATED TEAMS

Regardless of whether you are integrating people into squads at the marketing level, the customer value level, or at the company level, there are six practices that allow you to develop and manage squads for optimal agility and market system health:

1. Orient around a customer-centric mission
2. Create a flatter, more flexible organization
3. Share power
4. Truly integrate; don't stop at alignment
5. Offer support services to squads
6. Nurture links and bridges

Some practice elements will seem familiar to modern leaders while others become necessary specifically in networks and may run counter to today's operation. Let's explore each of these six practices.

Practice 1: Orient Around a Customer-Centric Mission

Squad coordination is critical, and it starts with the mission. A mission is more than a goal. In his book *Team of Teams*, General Stanley McChrystal expressed the importance of fostering a shared consciousness among teams who work together. People make hundreds of decisions daily. Every decision moves squads closer or further away from their objective. Squad actions can't be scripted. Rules, processes, and metrics can be valuable assistants, but every VUCA situation is at least slightly different and requires innovation and problem-solving. If the North Star is clear, the mission will steer the team.

That North Star for multidisciplinary teams is having a *customer-centric* mission, not a mission that is company-centric. Missions must offer a clear perspective into the customer outcomes that the company aspires to achieve. Internal goals, especially financial goals, are important, and businesses must be financially sensible. However, internal goals are not the same as the mission. Jeff Bezos, founder and executive chair of the board at Amazon, states, "I strongly believe that missionaries make better products. They care more. For a missionary, it's not about the business. There has to be a business, and the business has to make sense, but that's not why you do it. You do it because you have something meaningful that motivates you."[6]

Great missions are motivating and constructed for the long term. They appeal to people's desire to be part of something larger than themselves. People want to work for companies whose purpose is intellectually and emotionally aligned with them. According to a Deloitte Insights study, purpose-oriented companies report 30 percent higher levels of innovation and 40 percent higher levels of workforce retention than competitors.[7] Examples of strong customer-centric missions or purpose statement at a company level include:

- *Alzheimer's Association:* The Alzheimer's Association leads the way to end Alzheimer's and all other dementia—by accelerating global research, driving risk reduction and early detection, and maximizing quality care and support.

- *Caterpillar:* We help our customers build a better, more sustainable world.

- *CVS:* We are on a mission to deliver superior and more connected experiences, lower cost of care, and improve the health and well-being of those we serve.

- *Ikea:* Our mission is to offer a wide range of well-designed, functional home furnishing products at prices so low that as many people as possible will be able to afford them.

- *LinkedIn:* The mission of LinkedIn is simple: connect the world's professionals to make them more productive and successful.

- *Northrup Grumman:* At Northrup Grumman, we define possible by pioneering technologies at the edge of every frontier and creating revolutionary technologies to connect, advance, and protect the U.S. and its allies.

- *Shopify:* Making commerce better for everyone.

Because missions are an essential component of the company's strategy (i.e., the "what" and "why" of the enterprise), leaders charged with strategy set the squad missions. The squads then determine the "how" and "when" of mission delivery since these elements must adapt to fit the changing situational context. Missions at a squad level inherit the core values signified by the company mission. One marketing squad oriented around helping customers learn about the company's solutions stated their mission as: "We engage in two-way conversations and do the hard work of figuring out what information customers find useful and delightful."

An entire squad shares a common mission. Squads work as a unit and should be accountable and rewarded *as a team*. Holding individuals or single functions responsible for outcomes is like holding the pitcher responsible for baseball game results. Because squads are multidisciplinary, companies run the risk that squad members with different roles or expertise may feel like they are beholden to a lesser, self-serving goal or that they conflict with each other. Consider the risks to the surgical patient if the nurse is primarily focused on cost control or the surgeon is anxious about making her quota. No individual or specific discipline should independently win or fail.

Practice 2: Create a Flatter, More Flexible Organization

Organizations need good managers to provide leadership and help with goal setting, planning, prioritizing, and other essential tasks. So a company without managers will stumble around. Companies that have experimented with no management usually end up adding the function back in. However, almost every organization can benefit from fewer people who see their job as only "managing." Here are some tips on how to make that happen.

Employ Fewer Managers

Flatter organizations (with fewer management layers compared to a hierarchy) accelerate information flow, and since speed is important for agility, every management layer must add real value. Here's an example of how just one extra layer of management adds four conversations that might not be needed if workers were directly empowered to make decisions.

- **Conversation 1:** Christopher brings an issue to his manager, Patricia.

- **Conversation 2:** Patricia discusses the issue with her peer manager, Kumar.

- **Conversation 3:** Kumar gets a view from his employee, Chantel.

- **Conversation 4:** Kumar then goes back to Patricia to convey agreement.

- **Conversation 5:** Patricia finally gives the okay to Christopher.

Fewer conversations improve information fidelity. The children's game of telephone illustrates how stories change with each telling. Each time a story is sequentially whispered to the next child in the circle, the teller inadvertently drops or embellishes detail until, after several versions, the tale is hilariously different from the start.

Organizational hierarchies tend to get loftier over time unless they are carefully watched. Two conventions to watch out for are title creep (the practice of inflating someone's title without a change in responsibility) and promoting someone to a management level as a perk for performance or in lieu of monetary compensation, which can result in managers with only a couple of reports or even none.

Encourage Flexible Boundaries

Roles are a finer-grained unit of work than titles or positions. A role describes expected responsibility and accountability. Every employee job is a collection of roles. For example, the employment site Indeed.com describes the roles associated with a digital marketing specialist as "helping maintain a brand by working on marketing campaigns . . . performing market research, strategizing with other marketing professionals, and creating content."[8] In traditional siloed organizations, a person's roles tightly bind to their position (e.g., their title, level, and departmental designation).

Roles and positions don't need to be irrevocably wired together. Roles can be created as needed and discontinued when the need no longer exists. In practice, roles don't frequently shift, but the culture should accept fluidity for when circumstances change. If one squad temporarily needs extra content, someone usually focused on operations could be drafted into the role. The digital specialist may have market research in their job description, but that role could temporarily shift to someone who is better equipped to conduct a particular study.

Viewing work through the finer-grain lens of roles improves performance. The highest performers in a role are 800 percent more productive than the average, according to the McKinsey State of the Organization 2023 report.[9] Yet, many companies don't know which roles are highest value. As a result, between 20–30 percent of high-value roles aren't filled with the most appropriate people. This fact doesn't surprise me. I've helped leaders stack-rank roles by contribution to mission value, then examined the qualifications of staff filling those roles. One invariable insight—some of the best people are assigned to inconsequential roles.

Practice 3: Share Power

Squads must be empowered to take necessary action without going up a chain of command. They need latitude to act in the moment. Surgical teams can't keep running back to a manager for permission to stop a bleed. Baseball teams can't wait for instructions on whether to throw the ball to first base or not.

Empowerment is different from decentralization, a state that leaders often fear. I was often asked by marketing leaders, "Which is the right organizational structure—centralized or decentralized?" The question of centralization vs. decentralization seems like a fork in the road, and our choice is to take one path or the other. However, this choice is a false paradox exacerbated by silos.

In VUCA situations, centralization doesn't work. In the book *Organize for Complexity*,[10] consultant and author Niels Pflaeging writes, "In dull, slow-moving markets, centralization of decision-making is efficient. The centre [the part of the organization deprived of direct market contact] solves problems and gives out orders—the periphery [the part of the organization with market contact] executes upon them. . . . In fast-moving markets, however, the center loses its knowledge superiority. Central steering and any system that relies on central decisions collapses. Such systems become dumbed-down and numb."

However, decentralization doesn't work either. Decentralization enables a quick, customized response, but when independent actors act exclusively of their own volition, the result is chaos: duplication of effort resulting in cost overruns and confusion leading to delays and paralysis, lack of coordination, and inconsistency.

What we learn from leaders in turbulent environments is that it is possible to forge a new path down the middle. Take the best from decentralization—what people close to customers at the edge know and are good at—then link and guide these squads with missions (discussed in Practice 1) and with the supportive teams that are discussed in Practice 5. When we release the rigidity of hierarchy and functionally specialized silos and enable multiple links, the paradox of centralization vs. decentralization resolves.

In a ComplexityWise organization, control is neither transferred nor delegated to squads, as it would be in a decentralized model. Instead, it is formally shared between squads and management, and decisions are made not simply by virtue of where someone sits in the organization but rather by the most qualified person or team. Authority is best situated with roles rather than positions or people, and jurisdiction must be made explicit. One example would be where a new hire whose primary role is business development is found to be familiar with a new marketing technology, so they might assume a pivotal decision role during a tech stack architecture project.

Although squads are empowered to make mission-related decisions without needing to go up a chain of command, their work is not a free-for-all. Results follow behavior, and when people are both empowered *and* accountable, they are more careful about doing the right thing. Leaders should clearly communicate to marketers their expectations while supporting conditions that foster accountability. Empowering teams with accountability—for both investment decisions and results—unleashes entrepreneurial spirit and improves the like-lihood that outcomes will improve over time.

Leaders in a network also share power with each other. In a hierarchy, a single manager holds all authority for their department. In a network, most employees participate in more than one team and can have different manag-ers for various roles. A content marketing specialist assigned to a squad will have a squad leader responsible for that marketer's performance. The same specialist might also belong to a content marketing guild with another man-ager responsible for human resource tasks, including expertise development and hiring. The guild manager would be considered the "solid line manager" for the specialist.

Practice 4: Truly Integrate; Don't Stop at Alignment

Integration is not the same as alignment. Alignment is a machine term. Merriam-Webster.com defines it as "the proper positioning or state of adjustment of parts (as of a mechanical or electronic device) in relation to each other."[11] Physical machine components must align if they are to work together because each has distinct, hard edges and can't intermingle. When organizations try to align teams, they do so because managers assume that different disciplines must stay in separate silos with distinct edges, like machine parts.

Organizations can and must be more fluid in VUCA situations. Of course, unless the whole company decides to integrate into a network, mar-keting leaders will need to align with some groups, but it's important to understand that alignment is not an equivalent alternative to integration.

Take the challenge of aligning marketing and sales, for example. These two groups, each sequestered in their silos, are frequently at odds. Alignment activities include trying to break down communication barriers and opera-tionally coordinating through a raft of service level agreements, complicated processes, and technology, then stamping out disagreements that never seem to resolve. The sales team feels perpetually under-supported, and the marketing team perpetually overworked.

No matter how much effort goes into alignment, teams suffer disconnections. Customer prospect selection is a good example. According to an analysis from LinkedIn, the targeting overlap between B2B marketing and B2B sales is only 16 percent of customers.[12] This gulf would not happen in an integrated team. For companies choosing to continue alignment rather than integration, the challenge is worsening. In this digitally dominant era, a salesperson is lucky to get 5 percent of customer attention, according to Gartner Research.[13] Salespeople are typically responsible for revenue outcomes they increasingly have less control over. Now, 83 percent of purchase activity consists of independent learning and internal consensus building, according to Gartner, and in most companies, it's marketing that has the most well-developed and highly needed digital skills. However, digital capability alone isn't enough either. Customers say they want more self-help, but when they get stuck or need a problem solved, a human helper must be ready to step in.

Squads that integrate skills that have traditionally been housed in both marketing and sales will offer substantial relief from this historically persistent challenge.

Practice 5: Offer Support Services to Squads

No squad can accomplish its mission without help from other company experts. Supporting teams provide vital infrastructure and governance for scale, coordination, efficiency, and improved performance.

In a network configuration, supporting teams are sometimes called core, center, or hub teams, and these terms may subtly imply dominance or eminence, but as earlier explained, centralization is not the model for a ComplexityWise organization. When your goals are agility and market system health, it's the success of the edge squads that must drive everyone. Here are some examples of support services you should offer to squads.

Core Teams for Coordination and Responsiveness

Effective marketing requires a huge and growing range of capabilities, some of which can be offered in a shared services structure. The deep expertise needed to supplement squads will be provided by core teams, often aided by external agencies. While flexibility is needed for local responsiveness, squad performance benefits if everyone shares enduring marketing elements such as long-term strategies, brand and messaging architectures, some creative, and customer tools (i.e., customer data, customer personas, customer journey maps).

As in the time layering described in chapter 4: Think Like a Navigator, these elements are part of the "remembering" layers of delivering customer value, while elements including campaigns and specific customer tactics are part of the fast-paced innovation layers driven by the squads. The squad's role is to problem-solve and respond to the dynamic customer world. Like the surgical team, squads benefit from having scalpels and monitoring systems at their fingertips. Sharing these elements increases coordination, and situating deep expertise outside of the squads reduces distraction from the main squad mission. Although the core teams tend to share more job responsibilities and functions than squads, they should not be allowed to become silos.

One example of a core team is marketing operations, which typically manages the business support of marketing, including finance, reporting, and the mechanics of ROI. A great operations team also helps marketing stay productive and lean by removing bottlenecks and excess bureaucracy (e.g., procedures, policies, constraints). As companies move toward a squad model that integrates aspects of marketing and sales, what is now marketing operations may be incorporated into what is often called revenue operations, which integrates marketing and sales operations. Importantly, an integrated operations team that supports the range of customer value must be balanced. This means that revenue operations can't be sales operations with a small side dish of marketing.

No organization would be complete without the indispensable teams serving the whole company, among them finance, IT, and human resources.

Progressive leaders of these core functions are devising new ways to support agility and market system health. To advance transparency, accountability, and optimization, one financial leader decided to use a budget "tax" strategy to encourage these attributes. Any team that accepted the offer to implement technology and methods (vetted by finance and IT) to improve their transparency, for example, got a budget boost of 15 percent for a minimum of three years, and only a catastrophic business reversal would void this agreement. If a team declined the offer, their budget was lowered by 10 percent for the same period. As expected, the financial leaders have not yet had a refusal, and the company has progressed many desired changes.

Technology is a significant contributor to why networked organizations can work. Technology enables organizations to scale and coordinate in ways that were unavailable to earlier managers. Without coordinating technology, the empowerment of squads, for example, would be impossible to manage except in the smallest companies.

Chapter 7: The Information System: Collective Intelligence provides a list of important contributions that information technology contributes to the ability to manage marketing in VUCA environments. In addition to the steering, organizational memory encoding, assistance in controlling sprawling elements, and improving communication, technology assists squads and networks. For instance, it can support community by reinforcing the trust and norms that help diverse groups work together. People who feel attached are more likely to act in ways that improve the team and further the mission.

To support agility and market system health, major technology systems should integrate and be shared across squads and teams, including applications such as collaborative planning and resource management, project management, workflow, and communications. The technology team specifically focused on supporting squads will be a specialist core team separate from overall IT but working in close partnership. A private 2018 study[14] conducted by IDC for a tech client found that the best practice is for marketing to lead the martech strategy, including needs assessment, evaluation, deployment, data science, analytics, and business process operations. The company IT team should lead in data management and governance as well as company data integration. In no situation should either team act unilaterally.

Practice 6: Nurture Links and Bridges

The secret sauce of an integrated organization is not found in the organizational chart but rather in the way it is managed. While conventional companies put most effort into managing the chart's boxes, in squads and networks, the links enjoy equal importance. People need ties to others outside their primary team to foster innovation, increase creativity, problem-solve, and form relationships.

Different kinds of links serve different purposes. Direct ties (1:1 interactions) build trust and encourage sharing of complex, hard-to-codify information. Indirect ties are broader, more casual relationships such as social networks and friends of friends. These work well for monitoring and discovering. Ideally, squad members will have several strong ties to the people they work with regularly complemented by weak (more casual) ties to many others. For squads, some types of links are especially important to nurture, including the following:

- **Communities of knowledge and practice:** Individuals within multidisciplinary squads need professional "homes" where they can learn and improve their expertise. Also known as guilds or communities of excellence, these communities provide stability and continuity as people move between squads or initiatives. Digital self-help cannot take the place of an expertise community. While codified information assists learning, there is a limit to digital effectiveness. The experts who create the tools don't always give codifying their best effort, and some kinds of knowledge just can't be passed on in this way. Apprenticeship is necessary when information is complex and tacit. In marketing, knowledge community examples include content capability teams, analytics capability teams, or digital media teams.

- **Formal groups:** Formal groups are purposefully assembled to achieve a specific objective. Squads are formal groups. Other examples of formal groups include groups of expertise guilds (sometimes called chapters), advisory boards, and development workshops for high potentials. Each year, IDC's management team would gather about thirty individuals from across their three divisions for a three-day training. The links I forged the year I participated remained useful throughout my time at the company and beyond.

- **Informal crosscuts:** Social capital can be built through informal groups where crosscuts of people can get together to explore something they care about. Examples include interest groups (e.g., sports teams, book clubs, technology interests, or skill building) and geography groups (e.g., team members who live in the greater Phoenix area).

TAKE THIS AWAY

Achieving agility and fostering the customer centricity that supports not only today's revenue but also builds market system health requires a way of organizing different from the traditional hierarchy of departmental silos. What is needed are integrated, multidisciplinary squads that are abundantly connected. Marketing leaders can make significant progress by forming these squads within their current departments. Even more can be accomplished if companies integrate edge teams into customer value squads and eventually into a company network. By removing barriers to the flow of information, ideas, and expertise, companies will optimize marketing's contribution.

To become more agile, do the following:

- **Orient around a customer-centric mission.** Rather than organizing around internally relevant functions, ensure each squad has an externally beneficial mission.

- **Create a flatter, more flexible organization.** Although some hierarchy will remain and management is an important function, fewer levels of management work better. Roles should be allowed to shift as needed for the job at hand.

- **Share power.** Squads must be empowered to take necessary actions with agility. To increase coordination, make them also accountable as a team for results. Designate authority in roles rather than positions.

- **Truly integrate; don't stop at alignment.** Alignment, where people stay in silos while attempting to coordinate through formal arrangement, will not achieve a sufficient level of effectiveness.

- **Offer support services to squads.** For squads to be most effective, they need the support of other teams providing other kinds of expertise. Technology is also a critical support service.

- **Nurture links and bridges.** Connections between individuals and teams must be just as actively managed as the people and teams themselves.

CHAPTER 9

THE WORK METHOD: AN AGILE OPERATION

Agile is an attitude, not a technique with boundaries.
An attitude has no boundaries, so we wouldn't ask
"can I use agile here," but rather "how would I act in the
agile way here?" or "how agile can we be, here?"

—**Alistair Cockburn,** *Agile Software Development:*
The Cooperative Game

I met Gian Carlo at a cooking school in Tuscany. As the head chef, he taught our class traditional Tuscan dishes like pasta e fagioli and home-made limoncello. What I found most fascinating about my time with Gian Carlo were his stories about being a chef on a luxury cruise ship. I had never thought about what it would be like not to make just one great meal for your family but instead to produce ten thousand four-star meals. Each guest might have a special requirement. One is a vegetarian; one is gluten-free; one wants to eat in their cabin. One wants to eat at 7 p.m. on the dot and another wants to nibble all day.

A fast-paced professional kitchen like the one on that cruise ship must operate in a way that achieves both culinary excellence and agility. Of course, chefs must create delicious food if they want diners to keep coming back, just like marketers must create effective campaigns to earn a customer's business. But in environments where agility counts, where speed, variety, and customization dominate, the challenge is twofold. Not only must the chef worry about whether your tiramisu is amazing but also how to make twenty kinds of dessert for dozens of palates, perfectly served, on-demand, twenty-four hours a day.

Marketers have this same twofold challenge. It's not enough to generate creative campaigns. Marketing's work must also serve a constantly changing, never-ending plethora of stakeholder requirements. This requires an agile operation.

To achieve both these objectives simultaneously—amazing offerings delivered with agility—a professional kitchen cannot operate in the linear way we would when following a recipe at home for a single-family meal. What Gian Carlo told me is that the cruise kitchen staff thinks modularly and over a broader time scale. They break apart meal preparation into smaller tasks and then rearrange cooking jobs. For example, they prepare much of the meal ahead of time. They make huge containers of mashed potatoes and partially cook dozens of chicken breasts. Then when you order, the kitchen staff finishes your meals in all these little frying pans. Stacks of them. Their purpose-built methods enable them to serve great food with agility.

Fortunately, marketers already enjoy access to a robust discipline that helps them operate with agility. It's called Agile Marketing, and it is adapted from a popular software development methodology. In this chapter, I discuss why Agile Marketing methods work better in complex situations than older conventions and highlight four practices you should adopt to improve the agility of your marketing operation.

PURPOSE-BUILT FOR AGILITY

Modern marketing faces predicaments like those of software development. As Scott Brinker says in *Hacking Marketing*: "The challenges of creating great software and the challenges of creating great marketing share increasing similarities in a digital world. They're both juggling an explosion of digitally powered interactions in a tornado of constant change and innovation."[1] Some of these shared challenges include:

- Multiple stakeholders with different agendas
- Changing needs and requirements
- Service demands that exceed resources
- Widely varying (and difficult to measure) returns on investment

Like with software development, many traditional methods used by marketers underperform under today's VUCA conditions. Agile (spelled with a capital A) teams use methodologies such as Scrum and Kanban to apply design, communication, project management, and decision techniques that are better suited for turbulent environments. Agile accepts—even welcomes—change. The goal of Agile methods is to increase speed and flexibility without sacrificing coordination or quality. At a very high level, Agile operations can be summed up as an iterative series of "do-confirm-adapt" mini-projects illuminated by transparency, very similar to the wayfaring concept described in chapter 4: Think Like a Navigator.

Marketing leaders are fortunate to enjoy access to a growing community of Agile Marketing practitioners and coaches to assist them with embracing this system of methods. To help understand why I am enthusiastic about the use of Agile Marketing to help meet marketing's VUCA challenges, it's useful to share some background on the Agile movement's origins.

Development of Agile Principles

Early generations of software developers depended on assembly line–like "waterfall" processes where work started with elaborate plans, then passed work like a baton from one specialist group to the next via formal acceptance gates. This type of a process was how I originally learned to create and execute marketing campaigns, and in many marketing organizations today, waterfalls are standard.

Waterfalls aim to control quality, cost, and time, and they can work fine if projects meet the following criteria: Required information is available in advance, completion time is ample, and change requirements are minimal. This description rarely fits software development or marketing. Staged linear processes fail regularly under VUCA conditions because new information constantly enters the game at unknown intervals, altering requirements. Project managers try very hard to control the situation and avoid the "scope creep" caused by drifting demands. But trying to control everything is a fool's errand in a VUCA environment. Hoping to avoid the burgeoning problems caused by change, some project managers discourage stakeholders from interfering along the way, thus missing critical signals and rendering deliverables virtually useless. Further, when a specialist at an early waterfall stage passes learnings downstream to the next expert (who usually reports to another silo), critical knowledge gets lost between hand-offs. Upstream specialists find it difficult to plan with the needs of the downstream specialists in mind because, despite extensive requirements gathering, they don't always know what might be needed.

Marketers experience this accuracy gap in the staged process of the marketing-sales funnel, and it contributes to the bickering between the two groups. This gap also degrades the performance of campaigns if they take six to nine months to develop and therefore miss a market opportunity.

Since waterfalls fail so regularly in VUCA environments, it's not surprising that innovative software developers came up with a replacement: Agile. Because marketing as a discipline is different from software development, Agile Marketing is not an exact duplicate of the development version, but the two methodologies share foundational elements.

Agile originated in 2001 when a small group of software development thought leaders met in Snowbird, Utah, to come up with an alternative to traditional methods. The result was the Manifesto for Agile Software Development[2] accompanied by 12 Agile principles.

The manifesto and associated principles emphasize people. This focus is appropriate given that software development (and marketing) is knowledge work. Six of the principles direct how teams should be shaped and managed. For example, principle #4, "Businesspeople and developers must work together daily throughout the project," speaks to the variety of skills needed and how closely people must work together. Principle #8, "Agile processes promote sustainable development. The sponsors, developers, and users should be able to maintain a constant pace indefinitely," promotes a human-scale work environment. Of course, everyone must occasionally work a late night, but poorly designed feast-or-famine work discourages employees as well as corrodes quality. Other people-oriented Agile principles guide team empowerment, rich communication, and self-organizing management structure.

Several principles advise work processes. These encourage customer centricity, design excellence, simplicity, iteration, and the right way to measure. I especially like principle #2: "Welcome change requirements, even late in development. Agile processes harness change for the customer's competitive advantage."[3] This principle speaks to accepting inevitable uncertainty and affirms the right for customers to define desired outcomes.

Experts in Agile Marketing caution that to gain optimal value from the methodology, companies should not cherry-pick just the parts of Agile they like. I agree with this conclusion, which is why ComplexityWise marketing goes beyond operational adjustments. However, for the purposes of this chapter, I focus on practical, operational methods.

Scrum is the most popular version of Agile, and other derivatives include Kanban, Scrumban, and Lean. The roles and rituals of Scrum are still the most well-known and extensively used. Rituals include the following:

- Sprints (short project iterations)
- Daily stand-ups (short meetings to review progress and identify blocks)

- Reviews (informal reviews of work at the end of a sprint)

- Retrospectives (formal review at the end of a project to contemplate what happened during the iterations and identify actions for future improvement)

Agile approaches have taken the software development world by storm and are now rapidly gaining traction in IT, marketing, and other functions. The application of Agile in marketing started to seriously take off around 2009–2010. According to the 7th Annual State of Agile Marketing Report,[4] 86 percent of companies surveyed plan to transition some or all their marketing teams to Agile, and of those currently using it, 83 percent report having a positive experience.

I'm a big fan of Agile Marketing and have incorporated many of its concepts into this book. This chapter is not intended to be a how-to manual on Agile Marketing; there are plenty of Agile Marketing coaches and experts who are far more expert than I am on the frameworks, rituals, and practices, and the list of useful books, newsletters, videos, and podcasts about Agile Marketing continues to grow. But I include the discussion of Agile Marketing in this book because its use can accelerate progress toward system agility and market system health. Agile's primary benefits are the following:

- **Better managing of shifting priorities:** A reality of marketing life is that you are perpetually asked for more. Regardless of the size of your budget, you never have enough time, staff, or resources to give all your stakeholders all they need. Agile helps increase productivity but, just as importantly, offers a great way to process the morass of requests. Agile marketers maintain a visible backlog along with information about resource constraints and justifications to set expectations.

- **Increased speed:** Agile methods help marketers shorten the time to get campaigns to market. Speed is a benefit when working with VUCA challenges because it reduces the time between information gathering, action, and getting feedback. However, Agile isn't always about speed, and speed for speed's sake or as a substitute for strategy is a poor practice.

- **Ability to adapt to changing needs:** Getting deliverables in front of stakeholders more quickly while incorporating feedback dynamically and continuously throughout a project cycle allows marketers to continually test the viability of what is being worked on to ensure fitness to changing needs and thus reduces the risk of missing the mark.

- **Improved productivity:** In the enduring quest for efficiency, marketing leaders constantly look for ways to do more with less or get more done with the same resources. Marketing organizations who use Agile methods get more done, in the same way the cruise kitchen with its modular approach can serve many more meals than if they tried to do things like a family kitchen.

FOUR PRACTICES TO GENERATE AN AGILE OPERATION

My overarching recommendation is to connect with the Agile Marketing community and start, ramp, or deepen an Agile initiative. Companies unfamiliar with the methods can start by discussing the original Agile principles described already.[5]

Rather than attempt to replicate the formal Agile Marketing literature, I've summarized four practices that are baked into the building blocks of an Agile operation, along with an explanation about why they work so well for marketing's VUCA reality:

1. Make things smaller
2. Orchestrate and coordinate
3. Iterate and reprioritize
4. Simplify

These practices, sometimes called by other terms, show up in Agile Marketing. Let's explore what they mean.

Practice 1: Make Things Smaller

Projects made up of small elements that are loosely connected have advantages in VUCA situations when compared to large, entangled, monolithic projects. Think of building with Legos. When work products are thoughtfully dissembled, then astutely linked, performance speeds up, output flows more easily, iteration becomes practical, and project content can be flexibly adapted.

Historically, many marketing projects have been architected as "big bang" projects where all elements are conceived of, created, and delivered as an integrated unit. One example of a big bang project is a mulitmillion-dollar global product introduction campaign with scores of deliverables to be planned, executed, and launched simultaneously.

One reason big bang project methods have prevailed is that marketing projects prominent in the past (i.e., mass media ad campaigns, printed direct mail, and catalogs) require long lead times and had high costs. Agency business models thrived on this configuration, and as often happens, the habitual practices remained even though the need for them has declined. Big bang projects are also interesting and exhilarating to work on. What marketing leader doesn't relish a splashy new brand refresh, for example? In contrast, small, evolutionary tweaks can feel routine. One technology service provider lived for years with just one white paper, twisting it a little here and there to update it. That seems kind of boring, doesn't it?

It doesn't matter if marketers prefer big bang projects or agencies make money on them, in complex situations where things constantly change, monolithic projects lose advantage. They don't deliver value until late in the project life cycle, and long gaps between requirements gathering and delivery increases the risk that the project will miss its mark. The longer the project stays in development, the more time-consuming and expensive alterations become. This can lead marketers to avoid useful midstream change. Monolithic projects contain many entangled interdependencies, which create complications that make work harder to understand and projects to become precariously brittle.

Fresh, imaginative creative can be essential to great marketing, and an Agile approach doesn't shun big events or campaigns. What needs shifting is how they enter the work stream.

Modularize deliverables

In an Agile operation, long, risky, big bang projects are strategically deconstructed into an assemblage of smaller components that can be more quickly and easily launched, tested, adapted, rearranged, reformatted, reused, and repurposed. Decoupled elements allow greater independence, allowing them to travel more freely and at differing paces instead of requiring them to march in tandem. Untangled elements can be reprioritized and changed with lower impact on the overall system. The marketing team striving for agility will iteratively develop a library of modular assets such as templates, stories, and graphics, and then assembles these in a stream of campaign releases. Deliverables can be reprioritized as needed within the backlog of possibilities. Components that hit the jackpot can be amped up. Elements that don't work can be postponed for adjusting or be abandoned. This not only makes projects more flexible but it also increases resiliency. Monolithic projects are brittle and fragile. If one decoupled element fails, it doesn't take the whole entity down.

Clearly not everything in marketing can be scaled down. Events and other time-anchored programs must synchronize many moving pieces, yet Agile marketers have found creative ways to deconstruct. Those elements with long time horizons, like event venues, can be booked well in advance, while quicker turnaround elements, such as digital signage and session content, can ride on the faster-changing content stream and sync up with the event train at the appropriate interval.

Use Time-Boxing

Marketers striving for greater agility find that limiting time-allotted tasks to short intervals has several benefits. This is called *time-boxing* and is a practice that establishes a fixed end date, ensuring that work keeps moving. A sprint, one of the Agile processes described already, is a short time-box—typically a few weeks. Because of the wide range of marketing project types, Agile Marketing practitioners have found that flexibility is needed in setting time-boxes. Tasks not completed within the assigned time-box are pushed to the next one. Within each sprint, priority work is completed ahead of nice-to-have work. Team planning and review meetings—where members can show their work, get feedback, and identify where they need help—are quick (often as short as fifteen minutes). These meetings happen frequently, often daily. Limiting task time helps avoid *Parkinson's law* (work expands to fill the time allotted). Time-boxing promotes faster time to feedback, and what is learned in each iteration improves the project's fit to changing requirements.

Practice 2: Orchestrate and Coordinate

Just as complete decentralization in an organization is a recipe for pandemonium, a bunch of unconnected project elements would also be a mess. One criticism of Agile is that it can encourage a short-term focus, and marketers can lose sight of the bigger picture. These risks are alleviated by orchestrating and coordinating small pieces by connecting them to a bigger system.

Link with Guidance

When I interviewed one of the largest social networks about their content marketing process, they told me that they were surprised about how much documentation was needed to coordinate the outcome. Among the guidance that marketers needed was information about voice, tone, and style requirements. They found that the content contributors just wanted answers to these basic questions and didn't want to make the same decisions repeatedly. A core group of content experts put quite a lot of work into supplying this documentation, but it paid off in overall marketing productivity.

Setting thoughtful standards requires balance. Keep things too loose and you suffer the penalties of decentralization. However, scripting work too tightly prevents squads from adapting to customers' variable contexts (i.e., cultures, seasonality, generations, business models, social tribes). Shared principles work better rather than strict recipes. As a marketing advisor, field marketing leaders complained to me about "brand police" who were more intent on enforcing rules about logo size than helping them drive business. What they really needed was information about the rationale for standards so they could balance coordination with context-sensitive choices.

Traffic laws are an example of "rules" that vary by context and strictness of enforcement depending on risk. A few rules, such as driving on a particular side of the road and stopping at stoplights, are strictly enforced and everyone understands why. For other laws, like speed limits, drivers can't get too far out of bounds without penalty, but exact adherence isn't typically required. And occasionally transgressions are excused. A driver who unexpectedly swerves to avoid hitting a child would be lauded even though they drove out of their lane.

Connect to a Larger Narrative

At its heart, marketing is storytelling. Customer-centric marketing requires that all marketing content contribute to an overall narrative arc that supports the mission. Context-specific content is necessary, but you don't want every campaign manager defining the narrative too narrowly. Instead, each element should add something critical to a persuasive, interesting, credible story that nudges the customer toward deeper engagement and higher commitment.

Agile Marketers use stories extensively, in the form of short, customer-centric descriptions of requirements. In software development, stories define the interaction of a user with an application. In marketing, they can define specific tasks that need to get done or the role of deliverables. For instance, a sales enablement tool might describe this story: "As a salesperson, I want to gain my prospect's trust with references tailored to their industry, role, and business problem." Useful stories identify the person performing a certain action (the salesperson), the functions that the actor can/must perform (provide tailored references), and what the actor hopes to achieve by executing the action (gain the prospect's trust).

The Agile Marketing team's backlog, which contains work to be performed, is usually in this short story format. Anyone can contribute to the stack of ideas and programs from which prioritized work is pulled. The story format of work elements helps ensure that work is produced in a way that stakeholders can accomplish something valuable and tangible (not just a vague, random element unattached to the rest of the work), and it's easier to validate the priority of chosen work.

Practice 3: Iterate and Reprioritize

An agile response to a constantly evolving marketplace benefits from getting projects out in the real world more quickly. Change in a system isn't always sudden and catastrophic. Most change in markets consists of tiny alterations that only over time can be seen to significantly diverge. This kind of dripping change can delude marketers into assuming things are staying the same. Thus, a campaign with a six- to nine-month development time can miss the mark.

With shorter feedback loops, marketers increase the probability of staying in sync with market evolution because fewer changes happen between the time you gather intelligence and when you act. Also, giving squads a bit of extra time allows them to test and experiment more and a chance to adapt if initial efforts don't get good results.

The primary practice to keep things flowing is *iteration*. A continuous stream of act-learn-adapt cycles is how to move forward when the path is uncertain, as is discussed in chapter 4: Think Like a Navigator. The practice of modularizing makes iteration easier and more flexible. Marketers aim to accelerate the cadence and increase the frequency of intelligence gathering, analysis, and action to reduce the amount of change that occurs between intervals.

Being a marketer means accepting the burden that you will never, ever, complete your to-do list. There is a never-ending list of possibilities to make things better. Salespeople have an insatiable need for support. Executives are always offering up ideas or changing the end game. Product teams clamor for more attention for their brilliant inventions. And customers, who are as varied as stars, tend to habituate to last year's improvements and ask, "What have you done for me lately?"

Agile marketers rely on their constantly reprioritized backlog of investment opportunities to manage this crush. With each work cycle (usually sprints) the backlog is reprioritized so the opportunities with the greatest impact rise to the top. The team shares the choices (along with the clear metrics and reasoning for allocation) and the remaining order with stakeholders, sometimes including customers. Prioritization reflects the changing context as well as worthiness of a project. Teams say no to projects that don't add much value to the mission.

Practice 4: Simplify

The #10 principle in the original set of Agile principles is to "maximize the 'work not done.'" That is, don't allow anything nonessential to creep into the scope of your work. This principle fits well with the business's desire for efficiency as well as reducing complexity. The world is complicated enough without marketers making it worse.

One area ripe for simplification is the number of elements a person or a team needs to think about. By reducing actions in play—such as reducing the number of items on the work-in-progress (WIP) list—marketers can reduce confusion, avoid delays from indecision and conflicts, make prioritization easier, and lessen decision fatigue. Whenever something new is added, it is prudent to ask the question, "Is it necessary?" and if the answer is yes, then a secondary question should be, "What can we drop to make room for this?" To improve agility, actively assess and eliminate unnecessary items, steps, rules, and variations.

Have a Few Clear and Crisp Principles

Complexity increases when smart, zealous marketing managers inadvertently create overly bureaucratic processes with complicated steps and hand-offs. When I was a marketing leader, some of my best team members struggled with this habit as they tried to make things work as well as possible. I used the mantra "Make a rule. Cut a rule." to avoid a buildup of excess bureaucracy. I've seen some CMOs build a termination date into almost everything, forcing marketers to proactively reinstate something if it's still needed (and it frequently isn't). These kinds of practices work great.

Detailed rules aren't always necessary or helpful. It is astounding how much effectiveness can emerge when humans act in accordance with a few simple principles. A 12-step program, such as Alcoholics Anonymous,[6] is an excellent example. Despite being completely self-organizing with diverse and strongly individualistic members, A.A. has turned a clear mission (help alcoholics), twelve simple rules, and a minimal operation (fostering conditions for interaction including meetings and sponsors) into a worldwide organization present in one hundred eighty countries and a membership estimated at two million.

The wisdom of simple principles guides people in a broad range of fast-paced, high-change arenas. For instance, gamers use simple rules[7] to stay fluid and adapt to inevitable shifts and surprises. Gaming principles can be amusing. One gamer recommends, "Go the wrong way first." Martial arts are another complex context where principles apply. I studied the martial art aikido for several years, and the sensei taught me that the first principle of self-defense is "don't be there," excellent advice suggesting that we avoid getting into dangerous confrontations if we can.

Some leaders think that their group is too complex for simple rules (such as those used in a 12-step program) and may think they must make a multitude of commands to get the outcomes they want. But some large, successful corporations depend on principles. Amazon, for example, is famous for its leadership principles,[8] which include "Customer Obsession: Leaders start with the customer and work backward. They work vigorously to earn and keep customer trust. Although leaders pay attention to competitors, they obsess over customers" and "Frugality: Accomplish more with less. Constraints breed resourcefulness, self-sufficiency, and invention. There are no extra points for growing headcount, budget size, or fixed expense."

Deriving inspiration from the original Agile Manifesto developed for software development, a group of Agile marketers got together to develop Agile principles and values specifically for marketing. A list of the values can be found in the *Sidebar: Agile Marketing Values*.

AGILE MARKETING VALUES

1. Focusing on customer value and business outcomes over activity and output
2. Delivering value early and often over waiting for perfection
3. Learning through experiments and data over opinions and conventions
4. Cross-functional collaboration over silos and hierarchies
5. Responding to change over following a static plan[9]

Used with permission from the Agile Marketing Manifesto Team

Deploy "Minimum Viable" Design

The concept of "minimum viable" is foundational in Agile methodologies. It directs teams to start with a basic but complete set of ingredients so they can get their project into the real world and get feedback flowing faster. Minimum viable projects have faster time-to-value and are lower risk under complex conditions.

To give you an illustration of this concept, imagine an entrepreneur starting a business that they hope will result someday in a chain of bakeries. A logical first step would be to make a first store successful.

To be *viable*, this first store must have everything necessary to serve customers in place before opening. It must have location, staff, inventory, systems, supply partnerships, marketing, and back-office capability. No entrepreneur would start a bakery chain by renting four locations and installing inventory systems but postponing staff until some later date. Yet, some companies approach projects this way. They work on only the easiest or most comfortable elements first and avoid what is difficult, then wonder why the project is slow or fails.

To be *minimum* viable guides a project team to seriously consider what is just enough to get going and get feedback. That first bakery doesn't need to wait until fifty items are on the menu. A few will do. What is minimum viable varies by project. The decision must consider what the *stakeholders* find necessary, not what the project team wants to produce. I once saw a gorgeous sales playbook from a well-known company containing thirty-two pages of beautiful tables, infographics, and careful prose. Most marketers would die to work on such a wonderful piece. But the salespeople weren't thrilled. They desperately needed a playbook but didn't use this one. Why? The first page they cared about was page eight, they had to sift through the other twenty-four pages to find the few nuggets they needed, and this book was one of six required to get the full set of plays for just one new product.

Once a project gets underway with a minimum viable start, it can be expanded through further iterations. Each round is supported by well-defined user stories and clear success metrics to indicate when the project is "done" at each repetition.

As a final comment about the practice of simplicity, note that while restraint is usually beneficial, sometimes an addition can be a significant improvement—but there is a price to pay for adding complexity, so it is better to ask the question before mindlessly expanding.

TAKE THIS AWAY

Marketers already have access to a robust set of methods for operating with agility: Agile Marketing. Marketing, like the software developers that originated Agile methodologies, juggles an explosion of digitally powered interactions in a VUCA environment of constant change and the need for innovation. Traditional project management approaches, especially the linear waterfall method, contribute to marketing's persistent problems. The operational aspects of Agile Marketing are the most famous and deeply adopted, although experts caution that implementing Agile operations without the requisite mindset is like "hanging an Agile leaf on a hierarchical tree" and will not get the best results. Agile Marketing helps marketers better manage priorities, speed up time to market, adapt to changing requirements, and improve productivity. My overarching recommendation is to connect with the Agile Marketing community to increase essential capabilities.

Here are some ideas to get you started down the Agile Marketing path:

1. **Make things smaller:** Work products that are strategically modularized allow for increased speed, practical iteration, and flexible adaptation. Limiting time for tasks keeps things moving and supports prioritization.

2. **Orchestrate and coordinate:** Linking modular work products improves coordination. A balanced amount of guidance in the form of shared standards and systems, along with connecting to an

overall narrative arc that supports the mission, pays off in productivity without sacrificing important customization.

3. **Iterate and reprioritize:** Getting work out into the world faster, getting quick feedback, and then iteratively adapting helps marketers stay better aligned with market and customer changes. Real world feedback must drive priorities, so formulating a transparent backlog that adapts as needed increases campaign accuracy and aids communication with stakeholders.

4. **Simplify:** The world is complicated enough without marketers making it worse. Remove what's unnecessary everywhere, including work-in-process lists and rules and standards, and clarify communications. Adopt the concept of minimum viable to your launch approach.

CHAPTER 10

THE CHANGE MANAGEMENT METHOD: LEVERAGE EMERGENCE

This spontaneous emergence of order at critical points of instability, which is often referred to simply as "emergence," is one of the hallmarks of life. It has been recognized as the dynamic origin of development, learning, and evolution.

—**Fritjof Capra,** *The Hidden Connections*

Marketing organizations are complex systems, just like external markets of customers and competitors. To take advantage of the mindsets and capabilities necessary to thrive in a VUCA world, organizations must change. Guiding that change in marketing, or in any group for that matter, will be improved if you consider the implications of system behavior that I discuss throughout this book. In particular, the power of emergence.

As marketing leaders, we've all been a part of organizational change initiatives. They are notoriously frustrating and mostly ineffective. It is commonly claimed that 70 percent of change initiatives fail, and while the source of this statistic is murky, few would dispute it. Leaders complain about how people resist change. The TikTok topic "Corporate Reorganization Funny" had 68.4 million posts available on the day I looked at it.

Yet, change happens every day all around us, mostly successful and mostly without trauma because change is the natural order of complex systems. The challenge for marketing leaders is how to guide change in a specific direction and make it happen in a relevant time frame.

The response to this challenge is mixed news. Remember the butterfly effect? In natural and social systems, change is asymmetrical. Small interventions can have enormous effect; significant efforts sometimes make little difference. Like everything related to complexity, exact results can't be predicted, and unforeseen obstacles will inevitably crop up. But so will unforeseen gifts! In short, leaders can't expect change to advance in a neat, straightforward way. Emergence, the natural way systems change, is powerful, pervasive, and it's also tricky.

As I talk about in this chapter, leaders can deploy strategies to leverage the seismic effects of emergence and avoid the derailment of their plans. To do so they must invest in the conditions for emergence and strategically intervene to sway the odds in their favor. Here's some good news: Leaders don't have to think this process all the way through and come up with all the answers. The organization will do most of the work.

THE NATURE OF SPONTANEOUS CHANGE

In chapter 2: Different Thinking, Different Actions, I introduce the systems phenomena of emergence. As a refresher: In a complex system, change emerges, bottom-up, generated by the interactions between system participants and what's happening in their environment. Joi Ito, former director of the MIT Media Lab, puts it this way in a blog summarizing his 2017 talk with the Aspen Institute: "Emergence is what happens when a multitude of things—neurons, bacteria, people—exhibit properties beyond the ability of any individual."[1]

Emergent phenomena are decentralized, no one directs them, and they are self-organizing, meaning that new patterns arise spontaneously. Traffic is a good example of emergent behavior. One Saturday evening, I was driving on the 680 Freeway in the San Francisco Bay area, coming home from a birthday dinner for my daughter. I expected to be home quickly when, up ahead, brake lights sparked, causing me to suddenly and reluctantly decelerate into the congestion that was forming. With this tiny action, I contributed to the emerging traffic jam which slowly snaked up the highway. There was no preconceived strategy to cause a traffic jam; no one was following any plan. I certainly didn't want to participate, but an environmental trigger, an accident, changed the situation and sparked the emergence of different behavior where everyone involved acted accordingly.

Any time people interact (which is constantly!), emergent behavior is a possibility. For marketing leaders, the message is this: You can put together elaborate strategies packed with well-planned-out tactics and events. You can try to demand that people change their behavior. But none of that will guarantee you will get the change you want. What generates new, emergent behavior in complex systems are two mechanisms: simple rules and feedback loops, phenomena I discuss in earlier chapters. By intervening with these two elements, leaders can influence emergent change. Here's how they work when it comes to leading a change initiative aimed at developing a ComplexityWise marketing function:

Simple Rules: Joi Ito explains that emergence happens "simply through the act of (individuals) making a few basic choices. Left or right? Attack or ignore? Buy or sell?" Humans have "rules" that direct many of our choices. These rules may be *biological* in nature, such as "eat when you are hungry;" they may be *cultural,* such as "buy gifts for loved ones at the holidays;" or they may be *practical,* such as "buy when things are on sale." My traffic jam emerged primarily because of two simple rules: "Don't collide with the car in front of you" and "look wherever the group is looking—something interesting must be happening."

Feedback Loops: Feedback happens wherever one interaction influences others. As discussed in chapter 4, feedback loops come in two flavors: reinforcing or positive feedback loops, which amplify the direction of the original action, or balancing or negative loops, which redirect the energy of the interaction.

In the next section describing practices, I explore how applying simple rules and feedback loops can drive change in marketing functions and how leaders can influence these phenomena to favor the changes they want to see.

FIVE PRACTICES TO LEVERAGE EMERGENCE FOR CHANGE

Although emergent behavior is self-organizing, marketing leaders have a role in guiding it. They can intentionally foster the conditions in which emergent change will likely occur through the following five practices:

1. Increase connectivity

2. Identify guiding rules

3. Instigate with a bit of chaos

4. Initiate a minimum viable project

5. Increase diversity of backgrounds represented on teams

Practice 1: Increase Connectivity

Emergence gets its power from interactions. This is why the first practice to leverage emergence guides leaders to increase connectivity within the organization to liberate this power. As examined in earlier chapters, connection is essential for anything to work well in a system—intelligence, teams, operations—and it plays a critical role in transformation too. Once people have the means to connect, leaders can cultivate practices related to the simple rules and feedback mechanisms that are at play in emergence.

In fact, I think of connectivity as the secret sauce in emergence. You can do everything else well, and still, change will crawl or halt if it can't spread. The most important connections are not those between leaders and the team but rather among the group members who work together to create their collective future. While leaders must signal new behaviors through their own actions and through messages, the most dependable models are peers, and it is these peer-to-peer social connections that will form the pathway for new ideas, practices, and behaviors.

Formal communication channels, such as presentations and training events, are necessary. Ideas for a variety of formal links are described in chapter 8: The Organization: Integrated Teams.

However, the most powerful channel for spreading change is the informal back channel—the organization's social network. Leaders must not forget about this mighty underground force. While people may turn to experts to be informed, they turn to each other to be persuaded. People "sell" changes to each other by communicating and imitating. People become convinced by getting peer validation that the new way will be successful for them. Peer validation creates the powerful emergent pull. Without the flywheel of the social network, change agents must try to push innovation, which will eventually burn them out. As one Agile Marketing expert in a very siloed organization where this wasn't happening put it, "I'm like Harry Potter and I have to be there with my magic wand for anything to happen."

Marketers will be familiar with how to fan the flames of messages in social networks as this is a key capability for modern marketing. Organizational social networks work the same way. News travels when the group's influencers talk about what's happening. Influencers may emerge spontaneously due to their personality, role, or previous experience. Alternatively, they can be recruited to be a part of a pilot or initiative squad. Either way, marketing leaders should identify and work with these trendsetters. If the innovation works for them, news of their experience will travel through social networks and spread the change.

Practice 2: Identify Guiding Rules

Everyone shows up in the workplace with a cargo load of rules acquired from enculturation and prior experiences. Marketing organizations that have been together for a long time share many, many rules, and these drive current behavior.

If during a change initiative people seem confused or stalled, it's likely they lack a clear picture of where they are supposed to go. There's an old saying in sales: "The confused mind says no." If you want people to evolve in a new direction, they'll need fresh orientation. Thinking differently leads to acting differently, and one source of new thinking can be obtained in the mind shift chapters in part II of this book. "Think like an investor" or asking, "What would an ecologist do in this situation?" make excellent maxims to steer decisions down new paths.

To increase the stickiness and transmissibility of new rules, leaders can embed them in easily remembered, easily shared communication tools. To illustrate this concept, I share a story that I witnessed of how one marketing organization shifted their beliefs and behavior.

A new marketing leader had inherited a hyper-siloed marketing team whose members were constantly at war with other company departments. With his fresh eyes, the leader saw that his staff was unaware of the needs of other groups. They weren't bad people, but in their ignorance, they assumed they were doing the right things and therefore it was the others' fault that things weren't working.

To expose this marketing team to reality, the leader pulled together an in-person workshop with representatives from the stakeholder departments, including sales, sales operations, finance, product, IT, and customer service. Then he asked the astute (and safe) question to this group, "What marketing terms do you think *other* people don't understand?"

The group began shouting jargon: "Content, MQL, SEO, conversion, brand, flat rate, TOFU." The list grew so quickly that the person taking notes on the big tablet at the front of the room could hardly keep up. Soon, the walls were covered with long lists.

The marketers were astonished. They used these terms daily on their dashboards, and in work requests, emails, collaboration applications, and presentations. They had no idea that the marketing function was so poorly understood. With this visceral and humbling example fresh in everyone's mind, the leader and I assembled small cross-functional groups to develop new ways of working together. Initial change in the marketing team's behavior was immediate, and over the next few weeks, new processes and even friendships emerged.

This experience gave the marketing team a few important new rules to keep in mind: "Listen to what other departments need" and "translate your terms." Further, these rules were embedded in communication vehicles that ensured their future use in behavioral choices.

To help develop, communicate, and embed new guiding rules in your marketing organization, here are three tips:

- **Use sticky stories:** That marketing team (and I) will never forget the story of what happened in that room. Stories are one of the most powerful tools for change. They are the primary method by which people make sense of the world. They provide a structure for remembering facts. They give meaning to information that would otherwise be mundane, and they travel easily between people. The previous story has the five attributes that Chip Heath and Dan Heath, authors of *Made to Stick: Why Some Ideas Survive and Others Die,*[2] say that sticky stories must have: They are simple (lists of marketing jargon were made), unexpected (who knew that people outside of marketing knew so little about the function!), concrete (the team had a list to prove what had happened), credible (the team witnessed it themselves), and emotional (the marketing team later admitted to feeling shame and sadness).

- **Create special language:** Sometimes things come to life only when you give them names. For this marketing team, the term "the list" became a shortcut for reminding them about the need for collaboration. The Berkana Institute,[3] an organization supporting communities who aim for transformative change, suggests naming your initiative as a first step toward notifying everyone that something is different.

- **Employ killer facts:** In this case, the length of the jargon list served as numerical proof that change was needed, and I've observed other outrageous, memorable "killer facts" that spurred behavioral shifts. One example: Marketers in the 2010s embraced a statistic about how B2B customers don't talk to salespeople until they are 80 percent through their buying journey, and this fact illuminated how companies needed to adopt digital marketing and ecommerce fast. Although this "fact" likely wasn't *literally* true, it spread because the statement was *figuratively* true in the sense that it illustrated the dimensions of digital media's effect on the commercial process.

Practice 3: Instigate with a Bit of Chaos

Systems, including organizations, don't evolve voluntarily. They are most likely to change when the environment imposes something that disrupts equilibrium, thus stimulating interactions that get those feedback mechanisms looping. Management consultants have called out the need for a "burning platform," that is, some compelling reason why the organization can't stay where they are. The sweet spot for disruption is just enough to shake things up a little but not enough that the organization devolves into chaos. In the prior story, the marketing leader shook his team out of their complacent assumption that they were right and everyone else was wrong by bringing them face-to-face with proof of the opposite.

Leaders need to understand that the patterns of interactions in an organization are likely to be resilient. Once an organization has been together for some time, relationships, power structures, cultural norms, and bureaucracy entangle. This limits the emergence of new behaviors and increases the chances people will fall back into old ways.

However, the seeds of agitation may already be present. For example, marketers may be unhappy about the current situation and desire something that works better. Other sources of disruption that can serve as motivation include technological innovations (such as AI), declining sales, or customer loyalty problems. In any case, to kickstart change, leaders must either find this bit of chaos or turn up the dial on the urgency.

Practice 4: Initiate a Minimum Viable Project

Once disruption engages the marketing organization's interest, leaders have the opportunity to channel the direction of that curiosity. Initiating a minimum viable project related to the desired change will serve to make tangible progress, work as a positive feedback mechanism by being a model for the new way, and accelerate the change motion.

Chapter 9: The Work Method: An Agile Operation introduces the concept of *minimum viable* as a foundation for increasing operational agility, and marketing leaders can use this same concept to boost emergent change. For a change effort, form a multidisciplinary squad to collaboratively develop the kernel of what will someday scale to a larger effort.

One company initiated a minimum viable version of customer value squads in their Southern European region. The regional sales manager was passionate about the necessity for sales and marketing to work together more closely, and the marketing leader was forward-looking, business oriented, and a good partner. Over a couple of quarters, these two teams together devised everything they needed to work as integrated squads. It worked. The company's C-suite perked up when this region outperformed their peers, and they set out to scale the model to the rest of the European regions.

Leaders need not go overboard trying to make a minimum viable project perfect. In fact, perfection obstructs the value of minimum viability. But the first effort must be good enough to reasonably show results and to demonstrate value to others so that it can spread. By closely monitoring progress of the initial project, leaders can quickly step in to promote work in the desired direction and redirect work where it goes off course.

A minimum viable project will be a good way to start, but developing ComplexityWise marketing is a marathon, not a sprint. Leaders can use the iterative act-learn-adapt method of wayfinding, described in chapter 4: Think Like a Navigator, to scale the change effort.

In the case of the company devising integrated sales and marketing teams, once they saw how successful the Southern European region was, they analyzed why it worked and compared it to other teams working in more traditional ways. One critical success factor they identified was that managers needed the right mindset. So, their second phase was rolled out to the geographies with the most forward-looking managers. In other regions, managers with traditional mindsets stymied what executives had hoped would be a fast roll out. This challenge was frustrating but enlightening because it

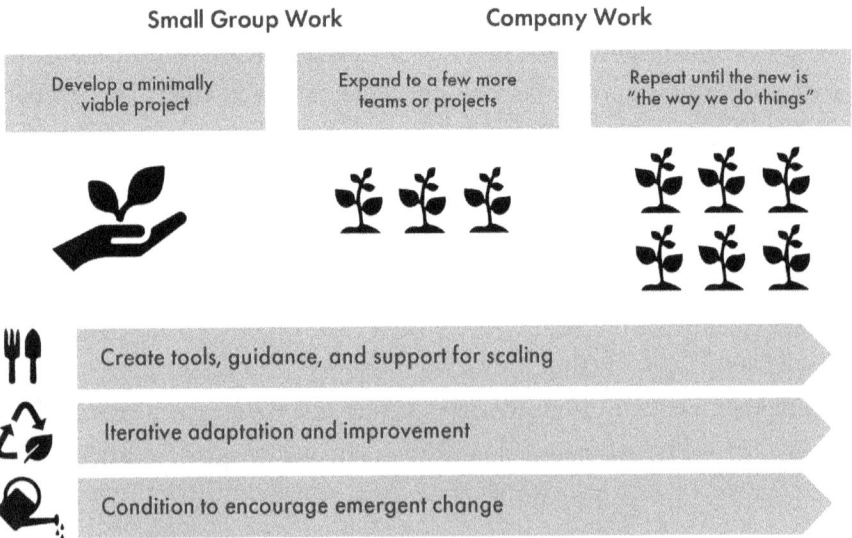

Figure 10.1: Scaling Change, from Small Groups to Company-Wide Work

gave leadership insight into the importance of having the right managers in charge of the future.

As a minimum viable project becomes a reality, marketing leaders must then invest in the tools, guidance, and support required to spread the capability (see figure 10.1). As shown in the figure, even though it is emergent, change still needs the resources and the means to come alive. Marketing leaders must ensure that the "supplies" needed for expansion (tools, guidance, support) are present, implement growth using iterative adaptation and improvement, and create the conditions for emergent change. Those factors, along with infrastructure for growth (including technology, mentoring, hiring, or assigning the right talent, expertise, and of course, funding) will allow what begins as small group work to evolve into company-wide practices.

Many marketers will be familiar with Geoffrey Moore's classic marketing tome, *Crossing the Chasm*,[4] and what he calls the "bowling alley strategy." Moore's work leverages systems thinking. He describes a strategy for growth that starts by winning a single niche market. That first niche win becomes the head pin in the bowling analogy. Knocking down that head pin provides momentum to topple nearby pins (or additional niche markets) until a company has captured huge market share. Think of your minimum viable project for organizational change as that head pin, and then select your next projects or teams from people adjacent in a significant way to the first. These adjacent teams will likely be the most connected to the first team and have the most robust social networks to spread the change. Learning from the initial project can become the model to mimic.

Company size makes a difference in the scaling strategy. Larger, more established companies will have the challenge of dismantling bureaucracies and an ocean of people to convince. However, some very large companies have made tremendous progress in ComplexityWise marketing and beyond. To give one example, a wealth management company with more than seventy thousand employees implemented multidisciplinary squads, which they called pods, representing their entire value chain—designers, developers, analysts, architects, marketing, legal, compliance, and more. The pods use agile processes, are self-sufficient, and enjoy the autonomy to generate ideas and make quick decisions. The company accomplished its objective to develop more personalized trading ideas for customers and lower the risk of offering these custom programs to clients, resulting in higher client activity, engagement, and positive feedback. Employees called the new work style "collaborative, challenging, and rewarding."[5]

Smaller companies, on the other hand, have a different problem. The good news is that small companies are natural networks and marketing leaders can use this to their advantage. Their size makes them speedy, tight-knit, able to pay close attention to their few customers, and animated by entrepreneurial spirit. Small companies can roll the bowling ball of change through the organization more quickly and with less effort. However, small companies likely lack enough people for all the needed ComplexityWise marketing capabilities. Small companies on tight budgets can fall into the trap of hiring marketing leaders who are too inexperienced (but cheaper) for the roles they've been assigned or deciding to forego essential elements such as intelligence. One solution is to supplement with deeper expertise from agencies, contractors, or fractional executive firms. Keep in mind, however, the need to find partners who are ComplexityWise or at least open to learning.

Practice 5: Increase Diversity of Backgrounds Represented on Teams

The outcome of emergent behavior is improved when individuals with diverse backgrounds (i.e., people from a variety of functions and with a variety of attributes) participate in its arising. As the organization evolves toward its collective future (especially in the early stages of change), they must solve unforeseen problems and invent new behaviors and processes that can't be planned for. Diverse perspectives will generate greater insights and innovation, thus increasing the chances that the group will figure out new ways that work. Broader skill sets will strengthen their ability to build new methods and tools. The company who devised their version of customer value squads could not have done so without both marketing and sales involvement.

Diversity also expands the communication routes for news and evidence of successful change to travel. Having a broader range of stakeholders involved also helps as change spreads. Although the principles of ComplexityWise marketing are universal, the details will vary in different situations. For example, the company further found as they rolled out their new squad model that they needed to adjust practices to accommodate the cultural differences in various regions.

At the beginning of a shift toward ComplexityWise marketing, many marketing leaders will find themselves stifled by traditional silos. Simultaneous to the minimum viable project (or in advance of), leaders can soften the boundaries between silos as a step toward increasing diversity and thus improving the speed and quality of emergent change.

Encouraging transparency is one action that softens the silo boundaries. Removing secrecy and allowing others to see inside and across departmental walls helps people understand how their actions affect the big picture. Change is less likely to be surprising when people have greater awareness.

Employees in bridge roles can serve as go-betweens and knowledge brokers to help different groups understand each other. Individuals with knowledge of multiple spheres can facilitate interactions and bring freshness into a staid group. Some examples include business analysts who work between marketers and data scientists, product marketers who understand both marketing and product domains, and partner marketers who work between marketing and external retailers.

TAKE THIS AWAY

Because marketing organizations are complex systems, they are subject to the same effects as customer markets. In a complex system, change emerges from the interactions of individuals and their environment. Marketing leaders can't control emergent change, but they can steer. By intentionally fostering the conditions under which change will occur and deploying strategies to influence the behavioral rules and feedback loops that form the process of emergent change, leaders can guide the organization to a more favorable future.

You can take advantage of emergence by doing the following:

- **Increase connectivity:** Connections between individuals in a system are what cause emergent change to arise and spread. Leaders must foster connectivity and work with it, especially the extremely important informal social network.

- **Identify guiding rules:** Provide navigation in the form of simple rules, illustrative stories, and other communication tools so that people's decisions move in the direction of desired change.

- **Instigate with a bit of chaos:** Systems need a little disruption to get things moving. A compelling reason to dispel complacency combined with some environmental shaking will kickstart change.

- **Initiate a minimum viable project:** Working through a holistic "minimum viable" project enables the team to tangibly figure out effective new ways. Then expand iteratively to scale, breaking through barriers and innovating solutions as you learn and adapt.

- **Increase diversity of backgrounds represented on teams:** Change requires innovation, and teams with diverse perspectives generate more insights and equip the effort with broader skills. Diverse teams increase the chances of successful initiation and also expand the channels though which change can emerge.

FROM UNCERTAINTY TO OPPORTUNITY

*Luck is what happens when preparation
meets opportunity.*

—**Seneca,** *Roman philosopher and statesman*

You are lucky.

Tomorrow, something wonderful will unexpectedly happen. A prospective customer will hear a friend rave about your product. A nasty problem will pop up and the innovation required to solve it will open the door to a lucrative new strategy. A shift in the CEO's perspective will lead her to boost the marketing budget, and you'll be ready with just the right project. Tomorrow, millions of surprises will materialize in the great, big, messy, real world and open the door to millions of opportunities.

You are lucky because you will have prepared. Having given up the industrial-era illusion that the marketing can be a centrally controlled vending machine, you'll possess the mindset and the courage to roll with what emerges. Persistent challenges, including the striving for predictable ROI, will have faded to the background. Having invigorated your market system health, you will have earned your customer's trust and loyalty, giving you greater resilience. Your increased agility puts you in the desirable position of being able to turn the unexpected to your advantage. You are lucky because you are ComplexityWise.

ComplexityWise marketing grants leaders a new, more relevant sense of mastery. This power comes not from eradicating uncertainty but from activating it to work in our favor. We seek inspiration from environments where we have not only familiarity but also competence, such as investing in the stock market, navigating the highway, and playing on a synergistic team. Where new proficiencies are needed—maybe for you that's statistics, ecology, or Agile methods—you can rest assured that we are a species with an amazing capacity to learn. And we have new tools. Data and analytics permit us to see the world's complexity in ways that were hidden from previous generations of marketers and managers. We can use this insight to make a consequential difference.

The benefits won't stop with marketing. Our world faces dizzying turbulence, from climate change to large-scale conflict and inequality. Speaking to Harvard University graduates, Bill Gates encouraged, "Don't let complexity stop you. Be activists. Take on the big inequities. It will be one of the great experiences of your lives."[1] Marketing already plays a pivotal role in business. It's time to take off the industrial-era shackles and generate both commercial benefits and the opportunity to contribute to a higher purpose.

SUGGESTED READING

BOOKS

Brand, Stewart. *The Clock of the Long Now: Time and Responsibility, the Ideas Behind the World's Slowest Computer.* Basic Books, A Member of the Perseus Book Group, 1999.

Brinker, Scott. *Hacking Marketing: Agile Practices to Make Marketing Smarter, Faster, and More Innovative.* John Wiley and Sons, 2017.

Duke, Annie. *Thinking in Bets: Making Smarter Decisions When You Don't Have All the Facts.* Portfolio/Penguin Random House LLC, 2018.

Ewel, Jim. *The Six Disciplines of Agile Marketing: Proven Practices for More Effective Marketing and Better Business Results.* John Wiley & Sons, 2021.

Fryrear, Andrea. *Death of a Marketer: Modern Marketing's Troubled Past and a New Approach to Change the Future.* Corsac Publishing, 2017.

Hamel, Gary and Zanini, Michele. *Humanocracy: Creating Organizations as Amazing as the People Inside Them.* Harvard Business Review Press, 2020.

Hurwitz, Judith H. and Thompson, John K. *Causal Artificial Intelligence: The Next Step in Effective Business AI.* John Wiley & Sons, 2024.

Johnson, Steven. *Emergence: The Connected Lives of Ants, Brains, Cities, and Software.* Scribner, 2001.

Kahneman, Daniel. *Thinking, Fast and Slow.* Farrar, Strouse, and Giroux, 2011.

Kupor, Scott. *Secrets of Sand Hill Road: Venture Capital and How to Get It.* Portfolio/Penguin, 2019.

Laloux, Frederic. *Reinventing Organizations: A Guide to Creating Organizations Inspired by the Next Stage of Human Consciousness.* Nelson Parker, 2014.

Martin, Roger L. *When More Is Not Better: Overcoming America's Obsession with Economic Efficiency.* Harvard Business Review Press, 2020.

McChrystal, General Stanley, US Army Retired with Collins, Tantum; Silverman, David; and Fussell, Chris. *Team of Teams: New Rules of Engagement for a Complex World.* Portfolio/Penguin, a Division of Penguin Random House LLC, 2015.

Meadows, Donella H. (Edited by Diana Wright). *Thinking in Systems: A Primer.* Chelsea Green Publishing, 2008.

Mlodinow, Leonard. *The Drunkard's Walk: How Randomness Rules Our Lives.* Pantheon Books, 2008.

Pascale, Richard T.: Millemann, Mark; and Gioja, Linda. *Surfing the Edge of Chaos: The Laws of Nature and the New Laws of Business.* Three Rivers Press, 2000.

Pflaeging, Niels. *Organize for Complexity: How to Get Life Back into Work to Build the High-Performance Organization* (4th edition, 5th edition available on author's website). Betacodex Publishing, 2020.

Sharkey, Linda, PhD and Barrett, Morag. *The Future-Proof Workplace: Six Strategies to Accelerate Talent Development, Reshape Your Culture, and Succeed with Purpose.* John Wiley and Sons, 2017.

Surowiecki, James. *The Wisdom of Crowds: Why the Many Are Smarter than the Few and How Collective Wisdom Shapes Business, Economies, Societies, and Nations.* Doubleday, 2004.

Tetlock, Philip E. and Gardener, Dan. *Superforecasting: The Art and Science of Prediction.* Broadway Books, 2015.

Watkinson, Matt and Konkoly, Csaba. *Mastering Uncertainty: How Great Founders, Entrepreneurs, and Business Leaders Thrive in an Unpredictable World.* Matt Holt Books, 2022.

Zolli, Andrew and Healy, Ann Marie. *Resilience: Why Things Bounce Back.* Simon & Schuster, 2012.

ARTICLES AND PAPERS

Adamson, Brett. "Traditional B2B Sales and Marketing Are Becoming Obsolete." *Harvard Business Review*, February 2022. https://hbr.org/2022/02/traditional-b2b-sales-and-marketing-are-becoming-obsolete.

Ackerman, Stacy. *MarTech's Guide to Agile Marketing for Teams.* Martech.org, October 2021. https://downloads.digitalmarketingdepot.com/MTC_2110_AgileMkgt_Download.html.

Binet, Les and Field, Peter. *The 5 Principles of Growth in B2B Marketing: Empirical Observations on B2B Effectiveness.* The B2B Institute/LinkedIn, 2020. https://business.linkedin.com/content/dam/me/business/en-us/amp/marketing-solutions/images/lms-b2b-institute/pdf/LIN_B2B-Marketing-Report-Digital-v02.pdf.

Chan, Serena. "Complex Adaptive Systems." MIT, Research Seminar in Engineering Systems, 2001. http://web.mit.edu/esd.83/www/notebook/Complex%20Adaptive%20Systems.pdf.

Cruz, Guilherme; Driedonks, Boudewijn; Ellencweig, Ben; Fischer, Maximilian; Hernandez, Fidel; Klemme, Josh; Lewis, Molly; Valdivieso de Uster, Maria. "Future of B2B Sales: The Big Reframe." McKinsey & Company, November 2022. https://www.mckinsey.com/capabilities/growth-marketing-and-sales/our-insights/future-of-b2b-sales-the-big-reframe.

Gulati, Ranjay. "Silo Busting: How to Execute on the Promise of Customer Focus." *Harvard Business Review*, May 2007. https://hbr.org/2007/05/silo-busting-how-to-execute-on-the-promise-of-customer-focus.

Lepore, Jill. "Not So Fast. Scientific Management Started as a Way to Work. How Did It Become a Way of Life?" *The New Yorker*, October 5, 2009. https://newyorker.com/magazine/2009/10/12/not-so-fast.

Li, Quan; She, Zhuolin; Yang, Baiyin. "Promoting Performance in Multidisciplinary Teams: The Roles of Paradoxical Leadership and Team Perspective Taking." *Frontiers in Psychology*, 2018. https://www.frontiersin.org/journals/psychology/articles/10.3389/fpsyg.2018.01083/full.

Mankins, Michael and Gottfredson, Mark. "Strategy Making in Turbulent Times." *Harvard Business Review*, September 2022. https://hbr.org/2022/09/strategy-making-in-turbulent-times.

Reeves, Martin; Nanda, Saumeet; Whitaker, Kevin; and Wesselink, Edzrard. "Becoming an All-Weather Company." Boston Consulting Group.com, 2020. https://www.bcg.com/publications/2020/how-to-become-an-all-weather-resilient-company?linkId=106701198.

Sargut, Gökçe and McGrath, Rita Gunther. "Learning to Live with Complexity." *Harvard Business Review*, September 2011. https://hbr.org/2011/09/learning-to-live-with-complexity.

Sullivan, Tim. "Embracing Complexity." *Harvard Business Review*, September 2011. https://hbr.org/2011/09/embracing-complexity.

Tadajewski, Mark. "Paradigm Debates and Marketing Theory, Thought, and Practice: From the 1900s to the Present Day." *Journal of Historical Research in Marketing*, Durham Business School, Durham University, UK, 2014. https://www.emeraldinsight.com/1755-750X.htm.

Wheatley, Margaret and Frieze, Deborah. "Using Emergence to Take Social Innovation to Scale." The Berkana Institute, 2007. https://www.margaretwheatley.com/articles/using-emergence.pdf.

NOTES

INTRODUCTION

1. "Age and Tenure in the C-Suite," Korn Ferry, https://www.kornferry.com/about-us/press/age-and-tenure-in-the-c-suite/.

2. Stewart Brand, *The Clock of the Long Now: Time and Responsibility* (Basic Books, 2008).

3. Stewart Brand, "Reframing the Problems," The Long Now Foundation, February 11, 1999, https://longnow.org/essays/reframing-problems/.

4. Peter Senge, *The Fifth Discipline: The Art & Practice of the Learning Organization, Revised Edition* (Crown Currency, 2010).

CHAPTER 1

1. Nicholas Evangelopoulos, "Citing Taylor: Tracing Taylorism's Technical and Sociotechnical Duality through Latent Semantic Analysis," *Journal of Business and Management* 17, no. 1 (2011): 59, https://www.chapman.edu/business/_files/journals-and-essays/jbm-editions/jmb-vol-17-01.pdf.

2. Peter Drucker, *The Landmarks of Tomorrow* (Harper & Brothers, 1959). The term "knowledge work," referring to work done primarily with minds rather than bodies, first appeared in this book.

3. "Cane Toad Invasion," Cane Toads in Oz, https://www.canetoadsinoz.com/invasion.html.

4. "Who First Originated the Term VUCA (Volatility, Uncertainty, Complexity and Ambiguity)?," US Army Heritage & Education Center, December 6, 2022, https://usawc.libanswers.com/faq/84869. According to the US Army Heritage & Education Center, the concepts behind the term VUCA draw on the leadership theories of Warren Bennis and Burt Nanus. The acronym first appeared in military education documents in 1987.

5. "Helmuth von Moltke 1800–91 Prussian Military Commander," Oxford Reference,

from *Kriegsgechichtliche Einzelschriften* (1880). Although this quote is often used colloquially as "No plan survives first contact with the enemy," the literal translation is "No plan of operations reaches with any certainty beyond the first encounter with the enemy's main force."

6. Kathleen Schaub, "Marketing Is Not a Vending Machine: Rethinking ROI for the Complex Digital Era," KathleenSchaub.com, January 11, 2022, https://www .kathleenschaub.com/blog/marketing-is-not-a-vending-machine-rethinking-roi/.

7. Wouter Aghina et al., "The Five Trademarks of Agile Organizations," McKinsey & Company, January 22, 2018, https://www.mckinsey.com/capabilities/people-and -organizational-performance/our-insights/the-five-trademarks-of-agile-organizations/.

8. Jack Ewing, "Why Tesla Soared as Other Automakers Struggled to Make Cars," *New York Times*, January 8, 2022, https://www.nytimes.com/2022/01/08/business/teslas -computer-chips-supply-chain.html/.

9. "Fortune 1000 C-Suite Survey: 96% See Their Marketing & PR Teams as 'Unwilling or Unable' to Prove ROI; Increasingly, Top Companies Are Turning to Finance, Procurement to Lead the Effort," GlobeNewswire by Notified, October 22, 2018, https://www.globenewswire.com/news-release/2018/10/22/1624837/0/en/Fortune -1000-C-Suite-Survey-96-See-Their-Marketing-PR-Teams-as-Unwilling-or-Unable-to -Prove-ROI-Increasingly-Top-Companies-Are-Turning-to-Finance-Procurement-to -Lead-the-Effort.html/.

10. Robert Frost, "A Servant to Servants," *North of Boston* (David Nutt, 1914).

CHAPTER 2

1. "Find Your Essential: How to Thrive in a Post-Pandemic Reality," IBM Institute for Business Value, February 2021, https://www.ibm.com/downloads/documents/us -en/10c31775c6d40101.

2. John Muir, *My First Summer in the Sierra* (Houghton Mifflin, 1911), 110.

3. Donella H. Meadows, *Thinking in Systems: A Primer*, ed. Diana Wright (Chelsea Green Publishing, 2008).

4. "Iceberg Model," ecochallenge, https://ecochallenge.org/iceberg-model/.

5. Stephen Eldridge, "Cognitive Bias," Encyclopedia Britannica Online, https://www .britannica.com/science/cognitive-bias.

6. Patrice Gaines, "How Oprah's Confession Tumbled Out," *Washington Post*, January 13, 1995, https://www.proquest.com/docview/903277472?sourcetype=Historical%20 Newspapers/.

CHAPTER 3

1. A few marketing expenditures have such short shelf-life that they can be considered costs. The value of pay-per-click ads, for example, disappears the moment you stop paying for them. Arguably, there is some risk involved in all advertising as well as some supplementation to future brand value, but for these kinds of costs, both are minimal.

2. Correlations can be surprising. One company I advised found a strong correlation between deal conversion and buyers who had, months before, accessed web content about the company's service practices, a type of content that the company soon realized they needed to pay more attention to.

3. "Longest Running TV Commercial," Guinness World Records, https://www .guinnessworldrecords.com/world-records/longest-running-tv-commercial/.

4. Mathew Hughes et al., "Marketing as an Investment in Shareholder Value," *British Journal of Management* 30, no. 4 (2018), https://doi.org/10.1111/1467-8551.12284.

5. Morgan Housel, "Investing Is a Fascinating Business," The Motley Fool, August 30, 2016, https://www.fool.com/investing/2016/08/30/investing-is-a-fascinating-business.aspx.

6. Heather Brown, "What Is a 'Bear Market' and How Long Might It Take to Recover?," CBS News, June 16, 2022, https://www.cbsnews.com/minnesota/news/bear-market-explainer/.

7. CFI Team, "Modern Portfolio Theory (MPT)," Corporate Finance Institute, https:// corporatefinanceinstitute.com/resources/career-map/sell-side/capital-markets/modern -portfolio-theory-mpt/#/.

8. Evan Gorelick, "Yale's Endowment, Explained," *Yale Daily News*, October 24, 2022, https://yaledailynews.com/blog/2022/10/24/yales-endowment-explained/.

9. Performance success was based on a blend of business metrics, customer satisfaction, and other factors.

10. Kathleen Schaub and Warren Lane, "Management Secrets from the IDC Tech Marketing Benchmark Survey," IDC Research, Inc., May 2020.

11. Peter Lynch with John Rothchild, *One Up on Wall Street: How to Use What You Already Know to Make Money in the Market* (Simon & Schuster, 2000), 18.

12. Scott Kupor, *Secrets of Sand Hill Road: Venture Capital and How to Get It* (Portfolio Penguin, 2019).

13. Institute of Practitioners in Advertising, https://ipa.co.uk/.

14. "The 5 Principles of Growth in B2B Marketing: Empirical Observations on B2B Effectiveness," The B2B Institute and LinkedIn, 2021, https://business.linkedin.com /content/dam/me/business/en-us/amp/marketing-solutions/images/lms-b2b-institute /pdf/LIN_B2B-Marketing-Report-Digital-v02.pdf/.

15. "Short-termism," Oxford English Dictionary, https://www.oed.com/dictionary/short
-termism_n/.

CHAPTER 4

1. "Quotes," Dwight D. Eisenhower Presidential Library, Museum & Boyhood Home,
https://www.eisenhowerlibrary.gov/eisenhowers/quotes/.

2. "Scientific Method," Encyclopedia Britannica Online, https://www.britannica.com
/science/scientific-method.

3. Stewart Brand, *The Clock of the Long Now: Time and Responsibility* (Basic Books, 1999).

4. Occasionally, large shocks like clear cutting or fire will, of course, upset the whole system
right down to the slowest changing biome level.

5. Brand, *The Clock*, 36.

6. "How Does GPS Work?," NASA Science Space Place, June 27, 2019, https://spaceplace
.nasa.gov/gps/en/.

7. Michael Mankins and Mark Gottfredson, "Strategy-Making in Turbulent Times,"
Harvard Business Review, September–October 2022, https://hbr.org/2022/09/strategy
-making-in-turbulent-times/.

8. Marc Brodherson et al., "The Power of Partnership: How the CEO–CMO Relationship
Can Drive Outsize Growth," McKinsey & Company, October 26, 2023, https://www
.mckinsey.com/capabilities/growth-marketing-and-sales/our-insights/the-power-of
-partnership-how-the-ceo-cmo-relationship-can-drive-outsize-growth/.

9. "Why Do We Believe That Catastrophes Come in Threes?," ABC News, July 2, 2009,
https://abcnews.go.com/Technology/WhosCounting/story?id=7988416/.

CHAPTER 5

1. Daniel Kahneman et al., *Noise: A Flaw in Human Judgment* (Little Brown Spark, 2021).

2. John von Neumann and Oskar Morgenstern, *Theory of Games and Economic Behavior*
(Princeton University Press, 1944).

3. Good Judgment, https://goodjudgment.com/. Superforecaster is a registered trademark
of Good Judgment, Inc.

4. "Advertising, Promotions, and Marketing Managers," Occupational Outlook Handbook,
https://www.bls.gov/ooh/management/advertising-promotions-and-marketing
-managers.htm/ and "Occupational Employment and Wage Statistics," US Bureau of

Labor Statistics, https://www.bls.gov/oes/2023/may/oes410000.htm/. In 2023, the US Bureau of Labor Statistics said there were 13,183M people in sales and sales-related professions compared to 347,000 in advertising, promotion, and marketing.

5. James Surowiecki, *The Wisdom of Crowds: Why the Many Are Smarter than the Few and How Collective Wisdom Shapes Business, Economies, Societies, and Nations* (Doubleday, 2004).

6. Anna Schmidt, "Groupthink," Encyclopedia Britannica Online, October 17, 2024, https://www.britannica.com/science/groupthink.

7. Annie Duke, *Thinking in Bets: Making Smarter Decisions When You Don't Have All the Facts* (Portfolio, 2018).

8. Nick Bilton, "The American Diet: 34 Gigabytes a Day," *New York Times*, December 9, 2009, https://archive.nytimes.com/bits.blogs.nytimes.com/2009/12/09/the-american-diet-34-gigabytes-a-day/.

CHAPTER 6

1. Alan M. Webber, "Learning for a Change," Fast Company, April 30, 1999, https://www.fastcompany.com/36819/learning-change/.

2. Michael Hammer and James Champy, *Reengineering the Corporation: A Manifesto for Business Revolution* (Harper Collins, 1993).

3. Joseph White, "Reengineering Gurus Take Steps to Remodel Their Stalling Vehicles," *The Wall Street Journal*, November 1996.

4. Kim Rutledge et al., "Ecosystem," National Geographic Education, November 8, 2024, https://education.nationalgeographic.org/resource/ecosystem/.

5. Linda Sharkey and Morag Barrett, *The Future-Proof Workplace: Six Strategies to Accelerate Talent Development, Reshape Your Culture, and Succeed with Purpose* (John Wiley & Sons, Inc., 2017), 49.

6. Sharkey and Barrett, *The Future-Proof Workplace*.

7. Beth Jensen, "Rethink Competition in the Workforce," Stanford Graduate School of Business, December 3, 2019, https://www.gsb.stanford.edu/insights/rethink-competition-workforce/.

8. Niels Pflaeging, "Competition in Organizations: Is It Good—or Bad?," Medium.com, March 6, 2018, https://nielspflaeging.medium.com/competition-in-organizations-is-it-good-or-bad-d31ab0e2a8d5/.

9. "How Do Stereotypes Form and Can They Be Altered?" Northwestern Institute for Policy Research, August 25, 2015, https://www.ipr.northwestern.edu/news/2015/eagly -stereotypes-social-role-theory.html.

CHAPTER 7

1. "LGP-30: The Royal Precision Electronic Computer," Royal McBee Corporation, 1956, http://archive.computerhistory.org/resources/text/Royal_McBee/RPC.LGP -30.1956.102646223.pdf.

2. Scott Brinker, "2024 Marketing Technology Landscape Supergraphic," chiefmartec.com, May 7, 2024, https://chiefmartec.com/2024/05/2024-marketing-technology-landscape -supergraphic-14106-martech-products-27-8-growth-yoy/.

3. Bill Schmarzo, *The Economics of Data, Analytics, and Digital Transformation* (Packt Publishing, 2020), 3.

4. Nick Bostrom, *Superintelligence: Paths, Dangers, Strategies* (Oxford University Press, 2016).

5. Judith S. Hurwitz and John K. Thompson, *Causal Artificial Intelligence: The Next Step in Effective Business AI* (John Wiley & Sons, 2024), xxix.

6. General Stanley McChrystal, *Team of Teams: New Rules of Engagement for a Complex World* (Penguin Publishing, 2015).

7. W. Edwards Deming, *The New Economics for Industry, Government, Education* (MIT Press, 2018), 65.

8. Amy C. Edmondson, *The Fearless Organization: Creating Psychological Safety in the Workplace for Learning, Innovation, and Growth* (Wiley, 2018).

9. Judith Hurwitz et al., *Augmented Intelligence: The Business Power of Human-Machine Collaboration* (CRC Press, 2021), 13.

10. Eva Ascarza et al., "Why You Aren't Getting More from Your Marketing AI," *Harvard Business Review*, July–August 2021, https://hbr.org/2021/07/why-you-arent-getting -more-from-your-marketing-ai/.

11. Eugène Ionesco, *Découvertes* (Editions d'Art Albert Skira, 1969).

12. Prompt engineering is the structuring of questions and supporting text to enable an AI to interpret inputs effectively and provide useful and accurate outputs.

CHAPTER 8

1. Andrea Alexander et al., "To Weather a Crisis, Build a Network of Teams," McKinsey & Company, April 8, 2020, https://www.mckinsey.com/capabilities/people-and -organizational-performance/our-insights/to-weather-a-crisis-build-a-network-of-teams/.

2. Kathleen Schaub, "Customer Value Squads: Empower Customer-Focused Teams While Avoiding Chaos," kathleenschaub.com, https://static1.squarespace.com /static/5eea412f206a1a190a96f4ef/t/643865f698404827de4fdc14/1681417723164 /CustomerValueSquads_KSchaub_April2023.pdf/.

3. "Welcome to Buurtzorg," Buurtzorg Nederland, https://www.buurtzorg.com/.

4. Karen Monsen and Jos De Blok, "Buurtzorg: Nurse-Led Community Care," *Creative Nursing* 19, no. 3 (2013), https://doi.org/10.1891/1078-4535.19.3.122.

5. "Home Care by Self-Governing Nursing Teams: The Netherlands' Buurtzorg Model," The Commonwealth Fund, May 29, 2015, https://www.commonwealthfund.org /publications/case-study/2015/may/home-care-self-governing-nursing-teams -netherlands-buurtzorg-model/.

6. JP Mangalindan, "Jeff Bezos's Mission: Compelling Small Publishers to Think Big," *Fortune*, June 29, 2010, https://fortune.com/2010/06/29/jeff-bezoss-mission -compelling-small-publishers-to-think-big/.

7. Diana O'Brien et al., "Purpose Is Everything," Deloitte Insights, October 15, 2019, https://www2.deloitte.com/us/en/insights/topics/marketing-and-sales-operations/global -marketing-trends/2020/purpose-driven-companies.html/.

8. "Digital Marketing Specialist Job Description: Top Duties and Qualifications," Indeed, October 28, 2024, https://www.indeed.com/hire/job-description/digital-marketing-specialist/.

9. Patrick Guggenberger et al., "The State of Organizations 2023: Ten Shifts Transforming Organizations," McKinsey & Company, April 26, 2023, https://www.mckinsey .com/capabilities/people-and-organizational-performance/our-insights/the-state-of -organizations-2023/.

10. Niels Pflaeging, *Organize for Complexity: How to Get Life Back into Work to Build the High-Performance Organization*, 4th ed. (BetaCodex Publishing, 2020), 58.

11. "Alignment," Merriam-Webster Online Dictionary, https://www.merriam-webster.com /dictionary/alignment/.

12. Jon Lombardo and Peter Weinberg, "The 'Circles of Doom': Quantifying the Misalignment of B2B Marketing and Sales," MarketingWeek, September 28, 2023, https://www.marketingweek.com/the-circles-of-doom-quantifying-the-misalignment-of -b2b-marketing-and-sales/.

13. Brent Adamson, "Traditional B2B Sales and Marketing Are Becoming Obsolete," *Harvard Business Review*, February 1, 2022, https://hbr.org/2022/02/traditional-b2b-sales-and-marketing-are-becoming-obsolete/.

14. Kathleen Schaub and Dan Vesset, "CIO-CMO Collaboration: Essential for Elevating Customer Experience," March 2018. Disclosure: I was the coauthor of this study.

CHAPTER 9

1. Scott Brinker, *Hacking Marketing: Agile Practices to Make Marketing Smarter, Faster, and More Innovative* (John Wiley & Sons, 2016), xi.

2. "Manifesto for Agile Software Development," http://agilemanifesto.org/.

3. "Principles Behind the Agile Manifesto," http://agilemanifesto.org/principles.html/.

4. "7th Annual State of Agile Marketing Report," Agile Sherpas, April 2024, https://www.agilesherpas.com/7th-annual-state-of-agile-marketing-report/.

5. "The 12 Principles Behind the Agile Manifesto," Agile Alliance, https://www.agilealliance.org/agile101/12-principles-behind-the-agile-manifesto/.

6. Alcoholics Anonymous, https://www.aa.org/.

7. Jess McDonell, "10 Unwritten Rules of Gaming Everyone Knows," What Culture, November 22, 2023, https://whatculture.com/gaming/10-unwritten-rules-of-gaming-everyone-knows-2/.

8. "Amazon Leadership Principles," https://www.aboutamazon.com/about-us/leadership-principles/.

9. "Values," Agile Marketing Manifesto, https://agilemarketingmanifesto.org/values/.

CHAPTER 10

1. Joi Ito and Jeff Howe, "Emergent Systems Are Changing the Way We Think," Aspen Institute, January 30, 2017, https://www.aspeninstitute.org/blog-posts/emergent-systems-changing-way-think/.

2. Chip Heath and Dan Heath, *Made to Stick: Why Some Ideas Survive and Others Die* (Random House, 2007).

3. "We Go to the Edge & Push Forward," The Berkana Institute, https://berkana.org/.

4. Geoffrey Moore, *Crossing the Chasm: Marketing and Selling Disruptive Products to Mainstream Customers,* 3rd ed. (Collins Business Essentials, 2014).

5. Mike Dargan and Stefan Seiler, "Agile Isn't Just for Software Developers. It's a

Compelling Way for Companies to Work," Fast Company, June 15, 2022, https://www
.fastcompany.com/90760935/agile-isnt-just-for-software-developers-its-a-compelling
-way-for-companies-to-work/.

CONCLUSION

1. William H. Gates, "For What Purpose?," *Harvard Magazine*, July–August 2007, https://
www.harvardmagazine.com/2007/07/for-what-purpose-html/.

INDEX

Figures, tables, and endnotes are indicated by an italicized *f*, *t*, or *n* following a page number.

Author photograph by Aika Cardin Photography

ABOUT THE AUTHOR

KATHLEEN SCHAUB has spent her career at the forefront of marketing innovation, helping leaders navigate the ever-evolving business landscape. Now a writer and strategist, Kathleen draws on decades of experience to deliver fresh, practical insights for organizations seeking to thrive in complex markets.

Previously, Kathleen led the renowned CMO Advisory practice at International Data Corporation (IDC), where she advised hundreds of marketing executives—from Fortune 500 technology giants to ambitious start-ups—on building smarter, more effective operations. Before that, she served as a chief marketing officer and held senior leadership roles at top technology companies, gaining a unique, cross-functional perspective that spans the entire customer journey, from product marketing to sales.

Kathleen is known for her bold strategic vision, grounded in a solid understanding of what truly works in practice. With training in design thinking, knowledge of data and analytics, and a mindfulness-driven approach to leadership, she bridges creativity and science to generate actionable solutions. Her insatiable curiosity and gift for simplifying complex information make her an indispensable guide for leaders navigating today's challenges.

A sought-after speaker, Kathleen has keynoted marketing conferences, authored countless articles and research reports, and appeared on many podcasts and webcasts. She holds an MBA from Saint Mary's College of California and resides with her husband in the East Bay Area of California.

Learn more about Kathleen and her work at www.KathleenSchaub.com.

www.ingramcontent.com/pod-product-compliance
Lightning Source LLC
Chambersburg PA
CBHW031849200326
41597CB00012B/330

* 9 7 8 1 6 3 2 9 9 9 8 6 3 *